Small Business to Seven Figures

The 9 Scaling Principles to Turn Any Business into a Money-Printing Machine

Nathaniel Mathew

Biography

Nathaniel Mathew is dedicated to producing business and personal finance content rooted in extensive research and data-driven insights. By extracting knowledge from the most successful and authoritative sources—ranging from best-selling books to groundbreaking articles and industry-leading case studies—he ensures his work is backed by proven principles. Nathaniel's meticulous approach includes analyzing feedback from competitors' audiences to identify what readers value most and eliminate what doesn't work. This commitment to precision ensures every page is packed with actionable strategies tailored to real-world success, making his content a trusted resource for ambitious entrepreneurs and professionals.

Content

Introduction

In the early days of aviation, the Wright brothers, Wilbur and Orville, were two small-town dreamers fueled by ambition and creativity, operating a modest bicycle shop. They faced immense challenges without lavish resources or a team of experts. Yet, their tireless dedication was driven by a vision that once seemed impossible: human flight. Embracing an unconventional approach, they meticulously observed birds in flight and conducted hundreds of glider tests, seeking to master lift and control. When existing engines failed to meet their needs, they innovatively engineered their own lightweight powerplant.

On December 17, 1903, in the brisk winds of Kitty Hawk, North Carolina, they made history with a powered flight that lasted just 12 seconds and traveled 120 feet. This fleeting moment ignited the era of modern aviation. Today, the expansive global network of planes and airports uniting people and businesses across continents stands as a testament to their unwavering determination. The Wright brothers demonstrated that true success springs not from extraordinary resources but from exceptional resolve.

Every small business owner understands the relentless grind. You work tirelessly day in and day out, but somehow, the challenges keep multiplying. Trying to scale can feel overwhelming when you're juggling so many responsibilities on your own. Limited resources, the pressure to meet demand, and the desire to hire help while working within a tight budget can make the journey feel nearly impossible. When do you even find time for yourself? It's perfectly normal to feel the weight of that stress. But here's the good news: it doesn't have to remain this way.

This book is designed to be your supportive blueprint for change. "From Small Business to Seven Figures" is here to provide you with tangible tools and strategies to help you scale your business. There's no fluff—just practical steps that you can begin implementing right now. I wanted to make this book a short read and as straight to the point as possible because I value your time as a business owner. I want to respect your sacrifice for taking the time to read this book despite all the many things you need to handle in your business. So together, we'll explore 9 key principles that can help transform your small business into a thriving venture. This isn't just theoretical; it's a heartfelt guide from someone who understands the challenges you're facing and who has been through them.

The vision extends beyond just increasing profits; it's about creating a business that runs smoothly, allowing you to step back and focus on what really matters—growth and strategy. Imagine having a system in place that takes care of daily operations, freeing you up to dream bigger. This book will help you develop a self-sustaining model, addressing everything from financial management to building a resilient team.

What truly distinguishes this book is its real-world focus. You'll encounter compelling stories of entrepreneurs who have walked similar paths and found their way through the struggles. We will break down complex processes into manageable tasks, providing you with step-by-step frameworks to guide your journey. Plus, you'll benefit from the insights of successful entrepreneurs who have been where you are and emerged stronger.

You're not alone in this journey, and together we can navigate the challenges ahead. Let's turn those dreams of growth into reality.

Who is this book for? It's for entrepreneurs, small business owners, and anyone who's self-employed and tired of feeling stuck. It's for those who dream of scaling but don't know where to start. If you're ready to take your business to the next level, this book is for you.

What can you expect to gain? You'll learn how to build efficient systems that save time and resources, leverage technology to automate tasks, and create a strong company culture that attracts top talent. You'll discover strategies for marketing and brand building, even on a tight budget. And when the time comes, you'll have a clear path to exit strategies should you choose to sell your business.

The book is structured into easy-to-digest chapters, each dedicated to a crucial aspect of scaling. We'll dive into financial and time management, team building, leveraging technology, and much more. Think of it as your roadmap to success, with each chapter taking you one step closer to your seven-figure goal.

Now, I won't promise it will be easy. But I will promise it will be worth it. By applying the principles in this book, you can achieve transformative outcomes. You can build a business that not only thrives but also gives you the freedom and satisfaction you've been craving.

So let's get started. Your journey to a thriving, scalable business begins here. Embrace the change and get ready to transform your business—and your life.

Chapter 1: Dealing with Limited Access to Capital

Let's be real for a moment. Launching a business often feels like attempting to run a marathon with your laces tied together. You might have the vision, the determination, and perhaps an outstanding product or service, but then the harsh truth sets in: funding. Or more specifically, the absence of it. It can seem like everyone else has investors knocking on their doors with bags full of cash while you're stuck sifting through coins in your couch cushions. Trust me, you're not the only one in this situation. Every entrepreneur encounters the overwhelming challenge of figuring out how to finance their ambitions without unlimited resources. However, here's the bright side: many of the most prosperous companies began with little more than what was available at home. So let's discuss how to leverage what you have to your advantage.

Bootstrapping Strategies for Growth

Bootstrapping is the skill of transforming your spare change into a successful venture. It involves utilizing what you currently own, whether it's a few hundred dollars in savings or a garage filled with outdated equipment and maximizing it far beyond your expectations. The wonderful aspect of bootstrapping is that it encourages creativity and cost-saving. You learn to focus on decisions that keep your attention on what truly matters: your customers and your growth.

First and foremost, assess what you already possess. Your personal savings, for example, are an excellent starting point. I understand that tapping into that emergency fund might feel intimidating but view it as an investment in your future. You're placing a bet on yourself, and who's better to rely on? Then there's all the equipment you've previously acquired. Do you have a computer? Awesome, that means you already have an office. Own a car? Ideal for deliveries or client meetings. The key is to think outside the box with these resources.

One inspiring case is Nick Woodman from GoPro, who initiated his action camera business by selling shell necklaces from a van to raise funds for his prototype. Woodman dedicated every dollar to improving his product and promoting it, demonstrating that even with minimal resources, innovative funding and steadfast commitment can lead to the creation of a ground-breaking product.

Next, think about implementing a lean start-up model. This focuses on eliminating the unnecessary and honing in on the essentials. Ask yourself, what is the absolute minimum I need to get my product or service into customers' hands? Prioritize your fundamental product development. For example, if you're starting a bakery, concentrate on perfecting those unique pastries instead of rolling out a full menu from the beginning. Conduct budget-friendly market research. This doesn't entail hiring a pricey agency; instead, engage with potential customers, utilize online communities, or execute small-scale trials. You'll gather valuable feedback without depleting your finances.

Now, let's discuss revenue. The quicker you can start generating income, the better. One approach is to pre-sell your products or services. It's like enjoying your cake while having it, too. You receive funds in advance to create the products, and your customers enjoy the thrill of being first in line. Another possibility is to provide consulting based on your expertise. Are you skilled in social media? Perhaps a local business could benefit from your assistance in enhancing their online visibility. It's a beneficial situation: you profit while they develop.

And when those initial earnings begin to come in, reinvest them back into the business. I realize it's tempting to pocket that initial significant sale, but think about the long-term vision. Use those profits to finance product improvements or broaden your marketing initiatives.

Each dollar you reinvest into the business is a step toward scaling up. You're constructing a foundation for future growth, brick by brick.

Exercise: Take Inventory of Your Assets

Grab a sheet of paper and list everything you possess that could be beneficial for your business. Include financial assets, such as savings or a credit card with a low-interest rate. Note down your equipment, whether it's a laptop or a sewing machine. Don't overlook your skills —maybe you excel in graphic design or have a talent for numbers. This list serves as your starting point. It's your toolkit for bootstrapping your way to achievement.

Creative Financing Solutions

Let's face it—traditional bank loans can feel like applying for a mortgage on the moon. The paperwork alone is enough to make you want to crawl back to bed. But here's some good news: you don't need to rely on banks to get your business off the ground or take it to the next level. Creative financing solutions are like the secret menu of the business world. They're not exactly in your face, but once you know about them, you wonder how you ever missed them. Let's explore some of these alternative paths that can help you secure the funds you need without the red tape.

First up is **revenue-based financing**. This is a nifty little option where you receive capital in exchange for a percentage of your future revenue. Think of it like bringing a friend into the business who's only paid when you get paid. It's flexible, meaning that if business is slow, your payments are smaller. This can be a lifesaver for seasonal businesses or those with fluctuating income. The key here is that you don't have to give up equity or worry about fixed monthly repayments when times are tight.

Then there's the world of **peer-to-peer lending platforms**. These platforms connect you directly with investors who are interested in funding your business. It's like crowdfunding's sophisticated older sibling.

You pitch your business, and if investors like what they see, they'll fund your loan. The beauty of peer-to-peer lending is that the process is often quicker and less formal than traditional loans, and it can be a great way to build relationships with potential future investors.

Speaking of **crowdfunding**, this is a fantastic option if you have a product or service that can capture the public's imagination. Kickstarter, for example, allows you to raise funds from a broad audience by offering rewards or early access to your product. It's an excellent way to validate your idea and build a community around your brand. The trick here is to keep your backers engaged with exclusive updates and sneak peeks of what's to come. People love feeling like they're part of something special, and a successful crowdfunding campaign can provide that emotional connection.

Business competitions are another avenue worth exploring. These contests often come with cash prizes, mentorship, and publicity. You may need to polish your pitch to a shine, but the rewards can be substantial. Plus, the exposure alone can open doors to future opportunities. Many local and national organizations host these competitions, so keep an eye out for ones that align with your industry or niche.

Let's not forget **grants and subsidies**. While they might not be as easy to find as your favorite pair of jeans, they can be worth the hunt. Governments and private institutions offer grants for specific industries or innovative projects. If you're in tech, for example, there are grants specifically designed for startups working on cutting-edge technologies. The application process can be competitive, but a well-crafted proposal that clearly outlines the innovation and impact of your project can significantly increase your chances.

Resource List: Top Resources for Alternative Financing

1. **Revenue-Based Financing**: Companies like Lighter Capital and Clearbanc offer flexible funding solutions based on your future earnings.

2. **Peer-to-Peer Lending**: Platforms like LendingClub and Funding Circle connect you with investors eager to finance small businesses.

3. **Crowdfunding Platforms**: Kickstarter and Indiegogo are excellent choices for creative projects and innovative products.

4. **Business Competitions**: Check out local chambers of commerce or industry associations for upcoming pitch contests.

5. **Grants and Subsidies**: Websites like Grants.gov and SBIR.gov list federal grants available to small businesses and startups.

These creative financing solutions can be game-changers for your business. They offer the flexibility and access to funds that can help you grow without the heavy burden of traditional loans. It's about finding the right fit for your business model and goals. Embrace these options as tools in your entrepreneurial toolkit—they could be the key to unlocking your business's potential.

Building Partnerships for Financial Support

When it comes to building a business, the idea of doing it alone can feel quite appealing—like the independent adventurer charting their own path. However, the truth is that forming partnerships can be an incredibly valuable support system on this challenging journey.

Picture this: you own a small bakery, and just down the street, there's a cozy coffee shop nearby. You both cater to a similar clientele, and your offerings beautifully complement each other. By coming together, you can create delightful joint promotions, share marketing efforts, and even collaborate on events that not only bring in more customers but also foster a sense of community.

The right partnerships can enhance your credibility and broaden your reach, providing comfort in knowing you're not alone in navigating this complex landscape. Seek out individuals who align with your vision and values—like suppliers, fellow entrepreneurs, or local organizations. Finding partners who genuinely care about mutual growth can make a world of difference in your journey. Don't hesitate to network through local events, industry meetups, or even online communities that resonate with you. Remember, it's about creating connections that feel authentic and supportive. Additionally, consider collaborating on grant applications or funding opportunities. This approach not only strengthens your proposals, but it also showcases a united front and highlights the impact of your combined efforts.

Ultimately, embracing partnerships can provide you with a comforting network of resources and connections. By leaning on each other, you can navigate the ups and downs of entrepreneurship together, reminding you that you don't have to face the challenges alone. Together, you can achieve so much more.

A prime example of utilizing collaborations for significant scaling is the partnership between Red Bull and GoPro. Both brands embraced a common ethos centered around adventure, thrill-seeking, and pushing human limits. Red Bull, renowned for its energy drinks and sponsorship of extreme sports, discovered an ideal ally in GoPro, whose cameras are tailored to capture exhilarating moments.

Their collaboration went far beyond simple co-branding; it was a strategic alliance that harmonized their marketing and content strategies effectively. In 2012, Red Bull and GoPro revealed an exclusive global partnership, making GoPro the official camera for Red Bull events. This collaboration was not solely about having logos displayed on event signage—it was a unified vision. The companies joined forces to create dynamic content, such as Felix Baumgartner's historic space jump, which was co-sponsored by Red Bull and filmed with GoPro cameras. This event garnered millions of viewers around the globe and established an unforgettable connection between the two brands, solidifying their status as leaders in extreme sports and adventure.

The partnership boosted GoPro's brand visibility, associating it with the thrill and excitement that Red Bull already embodied, while Red Bull reaped the benefits of GoPro's advanced technology that enhanced its content production. This mutually beneficial relationship not only scaled both companies by broadening their audience reach but also enriched their brand identities. It serves as a testament to the effectiveness of partnerships in fostering mutual growth, demonstrating that aligning with partners who share your vision can elevate your business beyond what could be achieved independently.

Once you've zeroed in on potential partners, the next step is crafting agreements that are beneficial for everyone involved. This isn't the time for hardball negotiations or one-sided deals. Instead, think of it as setting up a friendship with clear boundaries. Maybe you agree on a revenue-sharing model, where both parties benefit proportionally from the partnership's success. Or perhaps you can barter services—your marketing expertise for their legal advice. The key is to ensure that the benefits are mutual, so both sides feel invested in making the partnership work.

Partners aren't just valuable for what they bring directly; their networks can be a treasure trove of opportunities. Think of it like this: your partner's customers are potential customers for you, and vice versa. By collaborating, you gain access to an entirely new and loyal audience. Consider joint marketing initiatives where you co-host events, cross-promote on social media, or bundle products together. These strategies not only increase your reach but also add a layer of credibility to your brand. After all, if another business is willing to vouch for you, it speaks volumes to potential customers.

Maintaining these partnerships requires more than just a handshake agreement and occasional check-ins. It's like watering a plant; it needs regular attention to thrive. Keep the communication lines open with regular updates and meetings to ensure everyone is on the same page. Celebrate joint achievements—whether it's a successful campaign or a new milestone. It's about creating a relationship that's more than just transactional. When partners feel valued, they're more likely to stick around for the long haul, providing stability and support as your business grows.

Remember that partnerships aren't just about financial gain. They're about learning, growing, and developing together. A good partner can offer insights and perspectives that you might not have considered. They can be sounding boards for new ideas, help you navigate challenges, or even provide mentorship. These relationships can be invaluable, especially in the early stages of your business when you're still figuring things out.

Building partnerships is like assembling a puzzle. Each piece may seem unrelated at first, but when you find the right fit, they create a bigger picture that's far more powerful than the sum of its parts. So, look around, reach out, and start building those connections. You might just find that the right partnerships can propel your business to new heights you never imagined.

Maximizing ROI with Limited Funds

Alright, let's get real about making every dollar work as hard as you do. We're talking about maximizing your return on investment (ROI) with limited funds. It's like squeezing the last bit of toothpaste from the tube—tedious but oh so satisfying when done right. The first step? Prioritizing high-impact investments. It's about finding that sweet spot where a little input gives you a huge output. Digital marketing is a great example. Compared to traditional methods like billboards that cost a fortune and reach who knows who, digital marketing lets you target specific audiences. You can reach that guy who's been googling "best coffee near me" with your new artisan espresso blend. It's personal, precise, and doesn't blow your budget.

Focusing on customer retention is another goldmine. It's more cost-effective to keep an existing customer than to acquire a new one. Think about loyalty programs or personalized email marketing. A repeat customer is like a friend who always shows up to your parties and brings a dish to share. They're invested in you, and keeping them happy pays off big time.

Now, onto cost-effective marketing strategies that pack a punch without emptying your pockets. Content marketing is king. I'm talking about blogs, social media, and user-generated content. Write about your industry, share tips, or tell your brand's story. People love a good story. It's not just about selling; it's about connecting. And social media? It's your stage. Share posts, engage with followers, and encourage them to share their experiences with your brand. User-generated content is like getting free advertising from your customers. When they post a picture of your product with a glowing review, it's more credible than anything you could say.

When exploring further strategies to overcome limited capital, one can look to the journey of Sara Blakely, the creator of Spanx. With just $5,000 in her savings and no formal education in business, Blakely carefully developed her initial prototype using basic materials, testing it herself prior to launch. Lacking the funds for a patent attorney, she took it upon herself to draft the patent application and managed early manufacturing and sales by canvassing door-to-door. This unwavering bootstrapping strategy attracted the attention of major department stores, launching Spanx into a billion-dollar enterprise. Blakely's journey illustrates how determination and ingenuity can turn a simple idea into a worldwide sensation, even when financial resources are limited.

This story highlights that for entrepreneurs grappling with financial limitations, the focus should not only be on maximizing a budget but also on leveraging creativity as a driving force for opportunity.

Operational efficiency is your best friend when funds are tight. Streamlining supply chain logistics means ensuring your processes are as lean as possible. Look at how goods move from supplier to shelf, and find those pesky bottlenecks. Automating routine tasks can also free up time and resources. Think of it as setting your business on autopilot for tasks that don't need constant supervision. Whether it's scheduling social media posts or automating inventory management, these changes can save money and sanity.

Tracking and analyzing investment performance is crucial to ensure you're not throwing money into a black hole. Use analytics tools to see what's working and what's not. If a marketing campaign isn't hitting the mark, adjust it. It's like cooking with a recipe; if the dish isn't coming together, you tweak the ingredients until it tastes just right. Stay flexible and be prepared to pivot as you gather data and insights. This approach ensures that every dollar you spend brings you closer to your business goals.

To wrap it up, making the most of limited funds requires a mix of smart investments, efficient operations, and data-driven decisions. It's about being strategic, not just throwing money at problems. With these tactics, you can stretch your budget further than you thought possible, maximizing ROI and setting the stage for growth. Now, take these insights and make them work for you. Your business deserves nothing less.

Chapter 2: Developing a Scalable Operating System

Picture this: you've got a great product, a loyal customer base, and a business that seems to be firing on all cylinders. But then, as you try to scale, it feels like everything is held together with duct tape and a bit of hope. Suddenly, the systems that worked when you were small just aren't cutting it. Orders get mixed up, emails go unanswered, and you're spending more time putting out fires than building your empire. It's like trying to upgrade a bicycle while you're already pedaling uphill. You need a plan—a blueprint for a business that can grow without falling apart.

Crafting your business blueprint is all about defining the core functions that make your business tick. Think of it as laying the foundation for a skyscraper. Without a solid base, the whole thing wobbles and eventually crumbles. Start by mapping out your key business processes. What are the essential steps that take a customer from interest to purchase? Document these processes clearly so you know exactly what needs to happen at each stage. This map is your guide, helping you see where bottlenecks might occur and how to streamline operations.

Next, identify your primary revenue streams. Where does the money come from? Maybe it's product sales, service fees, or subscription models. Understanding this is crucial because it tells you what to focus on and what to nurture. It's like knowing which plants in your garden need the most water. You feed what feeds you. And don't forget to recognize those critical customer touchpoints. Every interaction is a chance to impress or lose a client. Whether it's an email, phone call, or in-person meeting, make sure these touchpoints are consistently positive and aligned with your brand values.

With your business functions clearly outlined, it's time to establish some objectives. Not just any objectives, but clear, measurable ones that align with your long-term goals. This is where the SMART goals framework comes in handy. Your goals should be Specific, Measurable, Achievable, Relevant, and Time-bound. Imagine you're setting out on a road trip. Without a destination, you'll just drive in circles. Your objectives are the destination on your business map. They keep you focused and motivated, ensuring every move you make is a step toward your vision.

Let's take a quick look at Google. At its inception as a Ph.D. project by Larry Page and Sergey Brin, Google was far from the colossal entity it is now. Within their small dorm room at Stanford, they established the groundwork for an operating system that emphasized efficiency and scalability. The pair created the PageRank algorithm, which structured web results in a manner capable of accommodating rapid growth. As their user base increased, they emphasized modular development, ensuring that each system could grow without compromising the core architecture. This methodology facilitated the transformation of a basic search engine into a diverse empire. The takeaway? Constructing processes with future scalability in mind can pave the way for extraordinary growth.

Now, let's talk about developing a systematic approach. This is where you create structured systems that facilitate efficient workflows and decision-making. Think of it as putting the gears in place for a well-oiled machine. Use process documentation templates to lay out each task and procedure. These documents are like recipes for success, ensuring that anyone can step in and keep things running smoothly. Additionally, create Standard Operating Procedures (SOPs) for critical tasks. SOPs provide a consistent way to complete tasks, reducing errors and saving time. They're the instruction manuals that keep your business humming even when you're not around.

But a good system isn't set in stone. It needs to be flexible and adaptable to survive in today's fast-paced business environment. This is where agile methodologies come into play. Agile isn't just for tech companies. It's a mindset that encourages adaptability and responsiveness. Break your projects into smaller, manageable chunks, and regularly review progress. This approach allows you to pivot quickly if something isn't working, without derailing the whole operation. Regular system audits are also essential. They're like health check-ups for your business processes, ensuring everything is working as it should and identifying areas for improvement before they become problems.

Exercise: Visualizing Your Blueprint

Take a moment to visualize your business blueprint. Draw a simple diagram that represents your core business functions, primary revenue streams, and critical customer touchpoints. Use arrows to show the flow of operations and note any areas that need improvement. This visual representation can help clarify your business structure and highlight where changes are needed.

Crafting a scalable operating system is like creating a living, breathing organism. It grows, adapts, and evolves with your business. It's not just about putting systems in place; it's about creating a framework that supports growth and innovation. With a solid blueprint, you can steer your business confidently into the future, knowing that you're prepared for whatever comes your way.

Designing Efficient Workflows

Envision your business as a meticulously orchestrated ensemble. Each segment symbolizes a distinct department, and when they all function cohesively, the outcome is stunning. However, if one segment falls out of rhythm, the entire performance suffers. This is where streamlining processes to enhance efficiency becomes essential. Picture your office on a hectic Monday morning when everyone is rushing to complete their tasks. Bottlenecks are evident everywhere—emails accumulate, orders become stalled, and meetings exceed their scheduled times.

It's pure chaos. Lean methodology serves as your conductor, assisting in pinpointing redundancy and waste within your operations. By removing these inefficiencies, you establish a workflow that operates smoothly, allowing you and your team to concentrate on what truly matters: delivering value to your clients.

Lean principles guide us to perceive redundancy as an adversary. Maybe you have three individuals tackling a responsibility that could be managed by one person, or you might be generating reports that go unread. It's akin to lugging around unnecessary baggage. By recognizing these redundancies, you can simplify your processes and decrease waste. The objective is to streamline workflows so that everyone is clear on their tasks and timelines. This not only conserves time but also alleviates frustration, enhancing the work experience for everyone involved.

To monitor tasks and guarantee nothing slips through the cracks, utilizing task management tools can be transformative. The era of sticky notes cluttering your desk or disorganized to-do lists is now behind us. Solutions like Trello and Asana provide a digital alternative that keeps your entire team aligned. They offer a snapshot of what needs to be accomplished, who is responsible, and when tasks are due. With Kanban boards, you can visualize your workflow by moving tasks from "To Do" to "In Progress" to "Done." It's comparable to having a personal assistant that keeps everyone organized and accountable.

Delegation is another powerful strategy in your toolkit. As a business owner, the urge to do everything independently is understandable. You're accustomed to taking on multiple roles, but effective delegation can be transformative. When you delegate tasks, you empower your team and foster trust. It's similar to teaching a child to ride a bicycle. Initially, you maintain a firm grip, but ultimately, you must release and trust them to pedal on their own. Delegation frameworks provide a systematic approach to assign tasks according to skills and availability. This not only frees up your time for strategic thinking but also allows your team to develop and excel in their positions.

To verify that your workflows are functioning at their peak efficiency, evaluating and analyzing performance is essential. Key Performance Indicators (KPIs) serve as your compass, indicating how well your processes are operating. They act like the dashboard lights in your vehicle, warning you of potential issues before they escalate into significant problems. By routinely assessing these metrics, you can identify opportunities for enhancement and make informed decisions. It's not solely about tracking figures; it's about comprehending their implications for your business and leveraging that insight to drive positive transformation.

Picture a restaurant kitchen during its busiest dinner service. Chefs are moving purposefully, each aware of their responsibilities and executing them impeccably. Orders are coming in rapidly, but there's no sense of urgency because everyone is functioning efficiently. The line cooks have organized their stations, the sous chef is managing the timing, and the head chef oversees the entire operation. That's the characteristic of a well-structured workflow. It's not merely about completing tasks; it's about doing them effectively, with minimal waste and maximized impact.

Now, reflect on how this concept applies to your business. Whether you operate a local coffee shop or a tech startup, having efficient workflows is crucial for successful scaling. They enable you to manage heightened demand without compromising quality. They offer you the adaptability to respond to fluctuating circumstances, whether it's a sudden uptick in orders or a new competitor entering the field. Additionally, they lay the groundwork for future expansion, ensuring your business can grow without losing its balance.

Establishing efficient workflows is not a one-off endeavor. It's a continuous process that demands diligence and dedication. It involves constantly seeking ways to improve, to achieve more with less, and to guarantee that every aspect of your business operates in harmony. By embracing lean principles, adopting task management tools, prioritizing delegation, and assessing performance, you can create a system that not only supports your current operations but also lays the groundwork for future success.

Constructing a Strong IT Infrastructure

Establishing a business without a solid digital foundation is akin to building a house on unstable ground; it may endure for some time, but when challenging conditions arise, you'll face difficulties. A dependable and robust IT infrastructure is not merely a luxury—it's a necessity. Cloud computing revolutionizes this aspect. Imagine having continuous access to your business data from anywhere, at any time, without the worry of servers malfunctioning like a car engine in the summer heat. AI has taken center stage in helping businesses operate more efficiently. Think of AI as your very own digital assistant, always ready to tackle those repetitive tasks that eat up your time. From sorting through endless emails to managing customer inquiries, AI can handle it. Imagine being able to focus on strategy and growth instead of getting bogged down in the mundane. It's like having an employee who never sleeps and never asks for a coffee break. AI tools can be set to perform tasks that would otherwise require hours of manual labor, saving you money and boosting efficiency. And when it comes to online advertising, AI can target specific audiences with precision, ensuring your marketing dollars aren't wasted on uninterested eyes.

In our increasingly digital world, cybersecurity is as crucial as locking up the shop at night. You wouldn't leave your front door wide open, right? The same goes for your business data. Implementing strong firewall and encryption protocols is your first line of defense against cyber threats. These measures act like a moat around your castle, keeping the bad guys at bay. But technology alone isn't enough. Regular security training for your staff is vital. Employees need to be aware of phishing scams and other tactics used by cybercriminals. Regular training sessions can keep security top of mind, making sure everyone knows how to spot a suspicious email from a mile away.

As businesses grow, so must their IT systems. Scalability is key. You need systems that expand with you, not hold you back like an outdated flip phone. Scalable server solutions and modular software systems are your best friends here. They allow you to add new functionalities or expand capacity without rebuilding from scratch. It's like having a wardrobe that grows with your clothing collection. Start small, but make sure there's room to add on as needed. Regular IT audits are essential for maintaining the integrity of your systems. They function like routine check-ups for your digital infrastructure, ensuring everything operates smoothly and efficiently.

Artificial intelligence (AI) goes beyond merely replacing manual tasks; it fundamentally changes how you conduct operations. It speeds up processes, allowing for quicker and more efficient task completion. For instance, AI-driven chatbots enhance customer support by providing assistance around the clock, addressing inquiries and resolving issues even when you're unavailable. This innovation brings customer service without the added pressure of overtime. Additionally, for those who rely heavily on data, AI equips you with decision-making tools capable of analyzing patterns and trends, offering insights that lead to wiser decisions. This isn't about predicting the future; it's about leveraging existing data to anticipate what may come next.

Targeted and retargeting ads elevate your marketing strategies. AI enables you to focus on the right audience, ensuring that your message reaches those most likely to engage with it. It's akin to having a billboard that only appears for individuals already interested in your offerings. This kind of precision not only saves costs but also enhances conversion rates, making your advertising budget more effective and less wasted.

In summary, a strong IT infrastructure serves as the foundation of your business. It underpins your operations, safeguards your data, and fosters growth. With the appropriate systems established, you can concentrate on what you excel at: building a flourishing business.

Creating a Feedback Loop for Continuous Improvement

Imagine running a restaurant where you never hear from your diners. Are they enjoying the food? Is the service up to par? Without feedback, you're essentially flying blind, hoping everything's okay but never really knowing. The same goes for your business, whether you're selling artisanal cheeses or digital marketing services. Establishing regular feedback mechanisms is your way of staying in tune with both your customers and employees. It's like having a direct line to the very people who keep your business ticking.

Customer satisfaction surveys are a straightforward method, providing insights into what's working and what's not. Keep them short and sweet—nobody likes a novel-length questionnaire. Ask the right questions to get the feedback you need without overwhelming your audience. On the flip side, employee feedback sessions create an open dialogue, allowing team members to share their thoughts and ideas. Hosting these sessions regularly fosters a culture of openness and trust, where employees feel valued and heard.

Now, gathering feedback is just the beginning. The real magic happens when you analyze this information and turn it into actionable insights. Think of feedback as raw data, like a chef receiving a basket of fresh ingredients. It's up to you to transform these ingredients into a delicious dish—or in business terms, improvements that enhance operations. Start by identifying patterns and trends within the feedback. Are multiple customers mentioning a delay in delivery times? Is there a common theme in employee suggestions? Use data analysis techniques to dig deeper and uncover the story behind the numbers. This process can reveal hidden opportunities for growth and areas that require immediate attention.

Once you have these insights, it's time to act. Implementing changes based on feedback is crucial to demonstrating that you value the input you receive. It's like baking a cake; you don't just gather the ingredients and leave them on the counter. You mix them, bake them, and create something new. Use iterative process improvements to make gradual changes, testing and tweaking as you go. Start small—maybe it's adjusting your customer service scripts based on feedback or tweaking your product packaging to reflect customer preferences. The key is to be responsive and proactive, showing your stakeholders that their voices matter.

Promoting a culture of continuous improvement involves making feedback a fundamental aspect of your business ethos. It's essential to encourage your team to perceive feedback as a growth opportunity rather than as criticism. This shift in mindset can significantly impact the workplace, fostering an environment where everyone is dedicated to improvement.

Recognizing those who provide feedback is an effective way to reinforce this culture. Whether through a shoutout in a team meeting or a simple thank-you note, acknowledging feedback contributors can enhance morale and encourage continued participation.

Establishing a feedback loop isn't solely about addressing problems; it's about creating a robust and resilient business. It involves being proactive, anticipating needs before they escalate into issues, and consistently striving for excellence. By implementing regular feedback mechanisms, conducting thorough analyses, and committing to continuous improvement, your business can not only meet but exceed expectations.

As these practices become ingrained in your operations, you'll notice that feedback transitions from being an afterthought to a vital component of your decision-making process. This transformation can lead to elevated customer satisfaction, greater employee engagement, and ultimately, a more successful and sustainable business. Keep this feedback loop active and dynamic as you move forward—it's a true reflection of your commitment to growth and excellence.

Chapter 3: Leveraging Technology and Automation

Imagine you're at a lively farmers' market, surrounded by vendors showcasing products ranging from honey to homemade jams. However, one stall captures your attention—a vendor utilizing a clever app on their tablet to handle payments, oversee inventory, and even provide digital loyalty rewards. While others are struggling with cash and paper receipts, they're swiftly completing transactions. This vendor has adopted technology and automation, transforming their small stall into a thriving mini-business. Now, let's discuss how you can replicate this success in your own venture by choosing the appropriate tech stack.

Selecting suitable technology for your business goes beyond merely keeping pace with competitors. It's crucial to align your tech selections with your unique objectives and operational hurdles. Begin by assessing your genuine requirements. Are you facing difficulties with customer management, or is inventory management causing you stress? Identifying these pivotal challenges will help direct you toward solutions that tackle your specific pain points. Consider it like finding the right shoes; you wouldn't wear flip-flops in a snowstorm, would you? Likewise, your technology should suit your business requirements perfectly. Your growth strategies should guide these choices, ensuring the technology you select facilitates your future progress, not just your current situation.

As you explore your tech options, a vast selection is available to you. For example, consider SaaS, or Software as a Service. It offers a range of cloud-based solutions accessible from anywhere, at any time—similar to renting a car rather than purchasing one. This method allows you to use technology benefits without being tied to a long-term contract. Conversely, on-premise solutions require buying and installing software on your own servers, giving you more control but sacrificing some flexibility and necessitating a significant upfront cost—much like buying a car outright.

Then there's the ongoing debate between cloud-based and traditional software solutions. Cloud software operates much like your favorite streaming service—constantly available and regularly updated. In contrast, traditional software resembles a DVD collection that gathers dust over time. Each option presents its own benefits and drawbacks, so your choice will hinge on your specific necessities and resources at hand.

When determining your tech stack, it's crucial to consider scalability and integration. You want solutions that can grow with your business, rather than becoming obsolete during times of expansion. Look for systems that feature APIs—Application Programming Interfaces—that enable different software applications to work together without issues. Picture it as having a universal remote control for all your devices. Additionally, a modular software architecture is incredibly beneficial, allowing you to add or remove features as needed without a complete revamp. This kind of adaptability ensures your technology can evolve alongside your business.

Finally, gearing up for future technological advancements is vital; it's not simply an option. Emerging trends like blockchain and the Internet of Things (IoT) are transforming various sectors. Imagine your supply chain being monitored in real time via blockchain, leading to improved transparency and efficiency. Or think of smart devices that can automatically reorder products when stock levels are low. These ideas aren't distant dreams; they are rapidly becoming realities. By staying informed and planning ahead, you can position your business to take advantage of these innovations as they arise.

Exercise: Tech Stack Reflection

Take a moment to write down the current challenges and goals of your business. Next, list the technologies you're currently utilizing. Are they helping you meet those objectives, or are they hindering your progress? Reflect on what tech solutions might bridge the gap. This activity will help clarify your requirements and guide your choices regarding your tech stack.

Choosing the right tech stack might feel overwhelming, but it's about discovering the tools that fit your business perfectly. With the right decisions, you can streamline operations, boost productivity, and prepare your business for long-term success. So, dive in and investigate the options, knowing that the correct technology can be a vital partner in your business journey.

Implementing AI for Operational Efficiency

AI is no longer reserved for cutting-edge companies or science fiction films. It's akin to having a super-effective assistant who is always awake and can manage multiple tasks effortlessly. Envision having a system that communicates with your customers clearly, addressing inquiries and resolving issues while you focus on more strategic matters. Natural language processing (NLP) makes this a reality, enabling AI to comprehend and respond to customer service queries as if it were a human. This technology can manage everything from straightforward FAQs to more intricate interactions, alleviating pressure on your team and enhancing customer satisfaction. It's like possessing a customer service team that operates around the clock. But let's not get carried away. AI is powerful, but it shouldn't run the show on its own. There's a delicate balance between automation and the human touch. Imagine a car with autopilot. It's great for handling the mundane, but you still need a driver to make judgment calls. The same goes for AI. While it can process data and suggest actions, human oversight is crucial to ensure decisions align with your business values and goals. This collaboration between AI and humans can lead to smarter, more informed decisions. To make the most of this partnership, train your employees to work alongside AI tools. This might involve upskilling your team to interpret AI-driven insights and integrate them into your strategic planning. Think of it as teaching your team to dance with AI, where both partners know their steps and work in harmony.

AI isn't a set-it-and-forget-it solution. Continuous monitoring and optimization are key to unlocking its full potential. It's like tending a garden. You don't just plant the seeds and walk away; you water, weed, and prune to ensure healthy growth. With AI, regularly evaluate key performance metrics to see how well it's doing its job. Is it improving response times? Boosting sales? Reducing errors? Regular updates and system checks are essential to keep your AI tools running smoothly and efficiently. This includes updating algorithms, refining processes, and ensuring your data is clean and accurate. It's about keeping your AI sharp and relevant, ready to tackle whatever challenges come its way.

Checklist: Monitoring AI Performance

1. Track key metrics such as response time, accuracy, and user satisfaction.

2. Schedule regular system updates to keep AI tools current.

3. Conduct routine audits to ensure data quality and integrity.

4. Gather feedback from users to identify areas for improvement.

5. Adjust AI strategies based on performance insights.

Implementing AI in your business can be a game-changer, offering operational efficiencies that free up time and resources for what truly matters. With the right balance of AI and human oversight, you can create a dynamic duo that drives your business forward.

Implementing Automation for Scalability

Think about your daily operations. How many times have you found yourself buried in repetitive tasks that seem to eat away at your precious time? This is where automation comes in as your business's secret weapon. Start by identifying processes that are ripe for automation. If you're spending hours sending out the same emails or updating social media, it's time for a change. AI-driven tools can manage email and SMS marketing campaigns with precision, ensuring your messages hit the right inboxes at the right times. Social media schedulers can keep your profiles buzzing with activity, even when you're off the clock. And let's not forget about customer support—AI chatbots can offer round-the-clock assistance, handling queries while you focus on bigger fish.

Content creation is another area where automation shines. With AI, you can streamline the drafting, editing, and optimization of content across various platforms. Whether it's whipping up a quick blog post or curating a stunning image gallery, AI handles it with flair. Inventory and order processes can also benefit from automation. Imagine a system that tracks stock levels, manages orders, and even predicts future needs—all without you lifting a finger. It's like having a diligent assistant who never takes a sick day. But automation isn't limited to these areas. Look for other opportunities where tedious tasks can be automated, freeing you up to tackle more strategic initiatives.

Data-driven decision tools are your new best friends in this automated landscape. They offer insights that guide your choices and optimize your strategies. Take targeted ads, for instance. By employing AI, you can ensure your ads reach the most relevant audiences, saving money and increasing effectiveness. Automated financial management tools can streamline invoicing, payroll, and expense tracking, reducing errors and saving time. CRM and sales automation software track leads, manage follow-ups, and provide valuable customer insights, creating a seamless pipeline from interest to sale.

Netflix's story is a prime example of using technology and automation to drive success. In the early 2000s, the company transitioned from a DVD rental service to a streaming giant by leveraging cutting-edge technology. Reed Hastings and his team foresaw the potential of streaming and invested heavily in developing a robust and scalable streaming platform that used algorithms to personalize recommendations for users. This automation of content suggestions not only improved customer experience but also kept viewers engaged longer, boosting retention rates. Netflix's use of predictive analytics to determine which shows would succeed—based on viewer data—allowed them to invest in original content like House of Cards and Stranger Things. This strategic move turned Netflix from an upstart into a leader in entertainment, showcasing how adopting tech early and effectively can reshape an industry.

Choosing the right automation tools requires some thought. You want tools that fit like a glove, addressing your specific needs without over-complicating things. Look for CRM software with strong automation features that match your business model. Workflow automation platforms like Zapier can connect various apps, automating tasks and ensuring everything runs smoothly. It's like having a conductor orchestrating a symphony of interconnected tools, each playing its part in harmony.

Integration is key. When new automation tools don't play nicely with legacy systems, it's like trying to fit a square peg in a round hole. Seamless integration, often achieved through APIs, ensures new solutions work smoothly with existing systems. This approach minimizes disruptions and keeps operations flowing without a hitch. Regularly evaluate the impact of your automation efforts. Return on Investment (ROI) analysis will help you understand what's working and what needs adjustment. Automation should feel like a helpful hand, not a cumbersome addition.

Automating for scalability is about freeing yourself from the mundane, allowing you to focus on growth and innovation. It's about setting up a system where the routine takes care of itself, leaving you with the headspace to drive your business forward.

Utilizing Data Analytics for Informed Decisions

Picture this: you're running a small coffee shop, and every day a diverse crowd strolls in, from college students pulling all-nighters to office workers grabbing a quick caffeine fix. But have you ever wondered what brings them back or why some just walk past? That's where data analytics steps in, turning those mysteries into clear, actionable insights. By collecting data through surveys or CRM tools, you can start to map out customer behaviors. Are they more likely to visit after a social media post? Do they prefer your seasonal specials over regular items? This rich tapestry of information can guide you in tailoring your offerings to match their preferences. It's like having a treasure map that leads you directly to your customers' hearts.

Once you've got the data, the real fun begins with advanced analytics tools. Platforms like Tableau and Power BI are your new best friends, transforming raw numbers into visual stories. Imagine a dashboard that updates in real-time, showing trends at a glance—from daily sales spikes to customer demographics. It's like having a crystal ball that reveals where the business is heading. These tools don't just sit there looking pretty; they empower you to make informed decisions on the fly. With a quick glance, you can spot opportunities you didn't know existed or pinpoint areas needing attention. It's not just about crunching numbers; it's about making those numbers work for you in meaningful ways.

Turning insights into actionable strategies is where the rubber meets the road. Say your data shows a dip in afternoon sales. Instead of shrugging it off, you might adjust your marketing strategy, perhaps targeting promotions at the sleepy post-lunch crowd. Or maybe your analysis shows a surge in mobile orders—time to invest in a more intuitive app experience. This is where data becomes your strategic compass, guiding you toward growth opportunities. It encourages you to pivot and adapt, ensuring you're always one step ahead in the competitive business landscape.

But all this data wizardry is only as good as the quality of the data itself. Enter data cleansing techniques, your unsung heroes ensuring that the information you rely on is accurate and relevant. It's about scrubbing away the clutter, like cleaning a window to let in more light. Regular audits of data sources keep everything fresh and reliable. Imagine trying to bake a cake with expired ingredients—not ideal. Similarly, outdated or flawed data can lead you astray. By keeping your data pristine, you ensure that every decision is based on a solid foundation.

In the end, data analytics is like having a backstage pass to your own business. It reveals what happens behind the scenes, offering insights that can transform your operations. With the right tools and a strategic mindset, you can turn data into a powerhouse of potential, driving your business toward success.

Automating Customer Engagement

Imagine running a bakery where every customer who walks in is greeted personally by their favorite barista, who happens to know exactly what they ordered last Tuesday and how they liked their coffee. Now, imagine having that same level of personalized service but on a much larger scale, stretching across emails, chat systems, and even text messages. That's the power of automating customer engagement. Start with email marketing campaigns. Automated emails can be set up to welcome new subscribers, send birthday wishes, or follow up after a purchase. They're like little digital assistants who remember all the important dates and details, making customers feel valued even when you're busy baking your next batch of croissants.

Chatbots are another game changer. They can handle inquiries 24/7, answering common questions or directing customers to the right resources. It's like having a customer service rep who never sleeps, ensuring your clients always have someone to talk to, even at midnight when they're craving your famous chocolate chip cookies. But let's not just throw any bot into the mix. Choosing the right tools for customer engagement automation is crucial. Platforms like HubSpot and Intercom are designed to streamline interactions, ensuring every message is timely and relevant. These platforms can integrate seamlessly with other systems you use, creating a cohesive communication strategy. SMS automation tools also deserve a mention here. They're perfect for sending quick updates or limited-time offers, catching your customers' attention in real-time.

Personalization is key to making automated interactions feel genuine. Without it, your efforts can come across as robotic or insincere. Use dynamic content in your emails to address customers by name or tailor messages based on their past interactions with your business. Segmentation and targeting techniques allow you to send the right message to the right person at the right time. It's the digital equivalent of recommending a new pastry to a customer who loved last week's special. These small touches show you're paying attention, making customers feel seen and appreciated.

Measuring the impact of your automated engagement efforts is like checking the pulse of your business. Are customers responding positively? Are they more engaged than before? Tracking customer satisfaction scores and analyzing engagement metrics can provide valuable insights. These metrics tell you what's working and where there's room for improvement. Maybe you find that customers love receiving personalized recommendations but are less responsive to generic promos. Adjusting your strategies based on this feedback ensures your engagement efforts hit the mark.

Reflection Section: Personalizing Customer Engagement

Take a moment to think about your last few interactions with customers. Were they personalized, or could they use a bit more warmth and relevance? Consider how automation tools could help you create more meaningful connections without sacrificing your time.

Automation in customer engagement isn't just about efficiency; it's about creating a seamless, personalized experience that resonates with each customer. With the right tools and strategies, you can build lasting relationships that keep customers coming back for more of what you have to offer.

Cybersecurity Essentials for Growing Businesses

Let's be real for a moment. You're hustling hard, building your business, and aiming for that seven-figure goal. But amidst the hustle, there's a silent threat lurking—cyberattacks. It's not just big corporations that hackers target; small businesses are prime prey because they often lack robust defenses. Imagine opening your laptop to find a ransom note instead of your desktop. That's the nightmare of a ransomware attack. Or falling victim to phishing schemes, where attackers impersonate trusted contacts to steal sensitive information. These threats can cripple a business faster than you can say "firewall."

So, how do you arm yourself against these digital invaders? It starts with the basics. Picture setting up a fortress around your data, beginning with firewalls and antivirus software. These are your first line of defense, blocking unwelcome visitors. Think of them as a locked door for the digital realm. However, even the strongest lock is useless if your passwords are weak. Implement secure password policies—long, random combinations that are tough to crack. Encourage everyone to steer clear of using "123456" or "password" (yes, people still do that).

Next, let's focus on your team. As much as you trust them, human error often proves to be a weak link in cybersecurity. That's why educating employees on cybersecurity is crucial. Imagine training sessions where your team learns to identify phishing emails and employs good internet practices. These awareness programs are like providing your team with a map in a digital jungle. To make it engaging, consider simulated phishing exercises. They serve as fire drills for cyber threats, preparing your crew to act quickly when the alarm sounds.

Preparation is key, so having a cybersecurity response plan is non-negotiable. Think of it as your emergency manual for when things go south. This plan should detail incident response protocols—clear, step-by-step instructions for containing and mitigating a breach. Regular cybersecurity drills keep everyone on their toes, ensuring that if a real threat hits, your team knows exactly what to do. It's the difference between a coordinated response and a headless chicken scenario.

Cybersecurity isn't a one-time setup; it's an ongoing commitment. Regularly update your security measures, adapt to new threats, and keep the conversation going with your team. Remember, in this digital age, being proactive is your best defense.

As we wrap up this chapter, remember that cybersecurity is not just a tech issue; it's a business priority. With the right tools and training, you can fortify your business against digital threats, giving you peace of mind to focus on growth. The next step is about managing your finances efficiently, ensuring every dollar supports your scaling ambitions.

Chapter 4: Building and Managing Teams

Picture this: It's a Tuesday morning, and you're juggling a dozen tasks at once. Your phone's buzzing with emails, and there's a growing to-do list staring back at you with the audacity of a cat demanding breakfast. You're the captain of this ship, but right now, it feels like you're navigating through a storm, and the only crew member is you. It's time to build a team, but the budget's tighter than your old jeans after Thanksgiving. Don't worry; we've all been there. Building a dream team on a budget is like piecing together a puzzle with a few missing pieces, but with a bit of creativity and strategic thinking, you'll find those pieces and make them fit perfectly.

Attracting Top Talent on a Budget

Let's begin by discussing employer branding. It represents the essence of your business—what drives it, what it believes in, and why someone would want to join. Creating a distinctive company narrative is essential. Think of it as the origin story of your business, similar to a superhero's beginnings. Were you motivated by a market opportunity or a personal passion? Share that experience with prospective employees. Individuals are attracted to stories they can connect with or find inspiring. Highlighting this narrative and your corporate culture on social media is vital. Platforms such as LinkedIn are not just for job postings; they serve as showcases for your brand's character. Share behind-the-scenes glimpses, celebrate team accomplishments, or articulate your values. This openness not only draws the right candidates but also aligns with your organization's principles and atmosphere.

You might ask, "How can I discover these exceptional candidates without spending a fortune?" By exploring budget-friendly recruitment avenues. Professional connections on LinkedIn are invaluable. Engage with industry-specific groups, share insightful articles, or simply initiate conversations. These networks contain professionals keen to connect and collaborate. Participating in online forums with thriving industry discussions is another clever strategy. It's akin to attending a trade show from the comfort of your home, mingling with others who share your interests and enthusiasm for the industry.

At times, compensation isn't the only factor that attracts talent. Providing non-monetary benefits can be just as persuasive. Imagine a flexible work schedule allowing employees to start their day with yoga or manage school runs without stress. Flexibility has become the new status symbol. Opportunities for career development are also appealing. People appreciate learning and growing, and offering workshops, training, or mentorship can be even more enticing than a salary increase. These benefits demonstrate that you prioritize your team's advancement, fostering loyalty and commitment that money cannot replace.

Engaging in community service is not only good practice; it also serves as an effective recruitment strategy. Organizing career workshops or partnering with local universities for internship programs enhances your brand's reputation and connects you with eager, fresh talent. It's like sowing seeds in a community garden; eventually, these relationships flourish into a network of skilled professionals who are familiar with and trust your brand. By engaging with the community, you cultivate a positive image and attract individuals who resonate with your company's mission.

Take a moment for introspection regarding your business journey. What motivated you to start? What core values guide your company? Write down these reflections and use them to develop an engaging story. Share this with your network to attract individuals who share your vision and values.

Building a team on a budget doesn't mean compromising on quality. It involves utilizing your brand, engaging creatively with potential hires, and providing value beyond just a paycheck. By emphasizing what distinguishes your company, you can draw in top talent that aligns with your vision and passion, laying a robust foundation for growth and success.

Visualize entering your office and feeling as if you've stepped into a second home. The atmosphere is filled with camaraderie, and your team is genuinely engaged in their tasks. This is the supportive work environment that encourages long-term employee retention. It's not just about perks like ping-pong tables or free coffee; it's about fostering an atmosphere where individuals feel appreciated and acknowledged. Regular feedback sessions are crucial. They provide an opportunity for open discussions where employees can express their thoughts and concerns without feeling unheard. Offering mental health resources is another essential support mechanism. Whether through counseling or stress management workshops, demonstrating that you care about their well-being fosters trust and loyalty.

In its formative years, Microsoft was characterized by a culture that Bill Gates meticulously cultivated. Gates held talent in high regard and was committed to hiring people who were more intelligent than he was. He famously devoted countless hours to interviewing candidates, ensuring they possessed the drive and creativity to align with the team's vision. One remarkable example was the recruitment of Steve Ballmer, who joined in the early days and eventually became a key player in guiding the company's sales and operations. Gates' philosophy of empowering his team cultivated a culture in which innovative ideas could flourish. The collective efforts of the team led to the creation of revolutionary products like Windows, which took over the PC market and marked a significant era. This strategy bore fruit as Microsoft expanded; their outstanding teams developed Windows and Office Suite, which revolutionized global productivity.

The collaborative atmosphere that Gates nurtured also involved rigorous brainstorming sessions known for their intense debates. These meetings encouraged engineers to think outside the box and meticulously enhance their concepts. This culture emphasized not only technical expertise but also the importance of fostering an environment where employees felt both challenged and motivated. By focusing on a combination of autonomy and accountability, Gates made certain that every team member contributed significantly to Microsoft's swift growth. This approach established a legacy of ongoing expansion and adaptability, ultimately transforming Microsoft into a global technology giant. The lesson? Investing in capable, dynamic teams and fostering a culture of learning and growth can enhance a company's influence and greatness.

Next, let's discuss how to keep motivation levels high. Employee engagement goes beyond a trendy term; it is the core of a successful team. Recognizing accomplishments, whether big or small, can be incredibly impactful. Acknowledging efforts through public recognition in meetings or personalized thank-you notes can boost motivation. And who doesn't enjoy a bit of fun? Organizing team-building activities brings everyone together, breaking the routine and strengthening connections. These enjoyable experiences remind everyone why they belong to this team and reinforce the ties that encourage their commitment.

Career development acts as the secret ingredient for retention. Individuals want to expand their skills, learn, and envision a future within the organization. Providing mentorship opportunities can be transformative. Connecting employees with experienced mentors not only aids skill development but also promotes a sense of inclusion. Outlining clear career advancement paths is equally crucial. It's like giving employees a roadmap for their future, demonstrating to them that there are clear opportunities ahead. Work-life balance is more than just a trendy phrase; it's a crucial factor in employee satisfaction. Implementing remote work policies gives employees the flexibility to balance their professional and personal lives. Whether it's working from home on a Friday or adjusting hours to fit family commitments, this flexibility can reduce stress and enhance productivity. Encouraging the use of vacation days is another important aspect. It's not just about taking time off; it's about recharging and returning to work with renewed energy and focus. When employees know their well-being is a priority, they're more likely to feel valued and supported, which increases retention.

Creating a culture of retention means integrating these elements into the company's core values. It's about building an environment where individuals feel connected, supported, and inspired to grow. When employees recognize they're part of something larger, and that their contributions are valued, they're more inclined to stay and thrive. It's not solely about keeping talent; it's about fostering a resilient and motivated team that's prepared to tackle future challenges.

Hiring A Virtual Assistant

Hiring a virtual assistant (VA) can greatly benefit small business owners aiming to scale efficiently. VAs are skilled remote professionals who can handle various tasks like managing emails, scheduling, social media management, customer support, and basic bookkeeping. One of the main advantages of adding a VA to your team is the increased efficiency. Unlike traditional, full-time employees who need office space, equipment, and benefits, VAs work remotely and are typically paid hourly or per project. This arrangement helps businesses significantly reduce overhead costs while maintaining or even enhancing productivity.

Virtual assistants often work from countries with a lower cost of living, which is a primary reason their hourly rates are generally lower than those of local contractors. Many VAs are based in places like the Philippines, India, and other regions in Southeast Asia and Eastern Europe. The lower wage expectations in these areas stem from different living costs, enabling VAs to deliver high-quality work at a fraction of the price of local contractors in pricier markets.

This cost advantage allows small businesses to tap into skilled professionals without the financial strain of local rates. For instance, a VA in the Philippines might charge much less per hour compared to a contractor in North America or Western Europe, despite offering comparable quality and expertise. Thus, employing VAs is an appealing and budget-friendly option for small businesses aiming to grow and enhance their operations.

VAs are particularly useful for solopreneurs, start-ups, and small businesses with limited budgets. They are perfect for those who recognize the benefits of delegation but aren't ready to commit to hiring a full-time employee. However, not all businesses will find hiring a VA advantageous. Companies that need specialized, industry-specific skills or an on-site presence may not benefit as much from VAs. Additionally, owners who find it difficult to communicate clearly or to delegate tasks might struggle to manage a remote team member effectively.

The benefits of hiring a VA include flexibility, as their work can scale according to your needs. Access to a global talent pool enables you to find specific skill sets that might be challenging to locate locally. Furthermore, since most VAs are independent contractors, business owners do not have to manage payroll taxes or employee benefits. On the downside, there can be challenges such as time zone differences that may affect real-time collaboration and the risk of miscommunication if expectations aren't clearly articulated. Taking the time to find a VA who fits well with your workflow and company culture can also be a process.

These VAs can be found on platforms such as Upwork, Fiverr, Freelancer, OnlineJobs.ph, Belay, Time Etc, Virtual Staff Finder, TaskBullet where you can browse profiles, post job listings, and hire based on your specific business needs and budget.

In summary, bringing a VA onto your team can result in significant efficiency and cost benefits. For owners who know what tasks to delegate and can effectively manage remote workers, a VA can be a valuable asset. While challenges do exist, approaching the decision to hire thoughtfully can aid in driving sustainable growth and help move your business closer to achieving that seven-figure milestone.

Outsourcing vs. In-House: Making the Right Choice

Imagine you're in your favorite diner. There's the chef, cooking up a storm, and the server, making sure your coffee is always topped up. Both are crucial, but the chef focuses on the core task—cooking—while the server handles the diners. It's a similar situation when deciding between outsourcing and in-house staffing. Start by evaluating your core versus non-core functions. Core functions are the heart of your business—those tasks that define what you do and set you apart from the competition. Non-core functions, like payroll or IT support, are necessary but not what makes your business unique. Knowing the difference helps you decide where to focus your in-house team's talents and where outsourcing might be more efficient.

Now, let's talk money, because let's face it, every penny counts. Outsourcing can be a lifesaver for small businesses operating on tight budgets. Think of it like hiring a specialist for a specific job without the commitment of a full-time salary. When you outsource, you tap into a pool of experts who might be out of reach otherwise. You're not just hiring a person; you're gaining access to specialized knowledge and skills. Plus, the savings are real. You're not paying for training, benefits, or office space. Virtual assistants are a great example. They can handle administrative tasks, customer service, or even social media management without you having to worry about providing a desk or dental insurance. This flexibility allows you to allocate funds where they're needed most, like marketing or product development. Platforms such as Upwork, Fiverr, Freelancer, Time Etc, and TaskBullet can also be used to outsource tasks, giving you access to a wide range of freelance professionals with various skills, allowing you to hire experts for specific projects or ongoing support based on your business needs and many are very affordable.

On the flip side, there's something to be said for keeping certain operations in-house. Picture a bustling kitchen where everyone knows their role, the rhythm of the work, and the culture of the place. In-house teams offer enhanced control over processes. You can directly oversee projects, ensure quality, and make quick adjustments as needed. There's also the added benefit of building a cohesive company culture. When people work together in the same space, they form bonds, develop a shared understanding, and create a unified team spirit. This camaraderie can lead to innovation as ideas bounce around and evolve in real time. In-house staffing is particularly beneficial for roles that require a deep understanding of your company's mission, values, and goals.

But why choose one when you can have the best of both worlds? Implementing a hybrid approach allows you to optimize operations by combining the strengths of both outsourcing and in-house teams. Consider outsourcing IT support while keeping customer service in-house. This way, your in-house team can focus on building relationships and providing personalized service while the technical experts handle the complexities of IT. During peak periods, flexible staffing solutions can be a game-changer. Outsourcing additional support can help manage workload spikes without the long-term commitment, allowing your in-house team to maintain their focus and productivity without burning out.

In this balancing act, it's crucial to assess your business's unique needs, resources, and long-term goals. By strategically deciding which tasks to outsource and which to keep within the company, you can streamline your operations and position your business for sustainable growth. Each decision should reflect your business's priorities, whether it's cutting costs, enhancing control, or fostering a strong company culture.

Developing Leadership Within Your Team

Spotting future leaders in your team is a bit like finding the diamond in the rough. It's not always obvious at first glance, but with the right attention, those gems start to shine. Keep an eye out for employees who show strong problem-solving capabilities. These are the folks who don't just bring issues to your desk but come with solutions in hand. They're the ones who, when faced with a challenge, roll up their sleeves and get creative. Encouraging initiative and innovation is key here. You want team members who are willing to step out of their comfort zones—those who see possibilities where others might see roadblocks. When someone suggests a new way to tackle an old problem, listen. It might just be the spark of leadership potential you've been waiting for.

Once you've identified potential leaders, it's time to nurture their growth. Providing leadership training and development is like watering those seeds of potential, helping them grow into mighty oaks of leadership. Structured programs are your friend. Think workshops on communication and conflict resolution. These sessions can transform how your team members interact, turning potential friction points into opportunities for growth. Leadership seminars and webinars offer another avenue for development, exposing emerging leaders to new ideas and strategies. These resources equip them with the skills needed to navigate the complexities of leadership, from managing team dynamics to making strategic decisions.

Mentorship is another powerful tool in your leadership toolkit. Assign experienced mentors to guide these budding leaders. It's like pairing a rookie boxer with a seasoned coach—the guidance, insights, and encouragement can make all the difference. Regular coaching sessions provide a dedicated time for reflection and growth, allowing emerging leaders to discuss challenges, seek advice, and set goals. This relationship builds confidence and competence, helping them transition from potential to performance.

Leadership isn't just about sitting in meetings or making big decisions; it's also about getting hands-on. Empower employees to lead projects. Delegate responsibility and give them the reins. It's like teaching a kid to ride a bike—you have to let go of the seat at some point. Allow them to lead meetings and presentations, giving them a platform to develop and demonstrate their leadership skills. This practical experience is invaluable, building their confidence and capability.

Leadership development is an ongoing process. It's about creating an environment where potential leaders can thrive, grow, and eventually take the helm. You're not just building a team; you're building a legacy.

Managing Remote Teams Effectively

Imagine running a business where your team is scattered across cities, countries, or even continents. There's no bustling office, no water cooler chats, and sometimes, no clue what time zone everyone's in. Welcome to the world of managing remote teams—where communication isn't just key; it's the whole darn toolbox. Establishing clear communication protocols is your first move. Daily check-ins via video calls can make all the difference. They're like morning coffee meetings, minus the commute. These moments keep everyone in sync, help address any concerns, and ensure that nobody feels like they're talking to an empty room. Tools like Slack or Microsoft Teams are your best allies here. They're more than just chat apps; they're lifelines in maintaining open lines of communication, allowing for quick updates and ongoing discussions without clogging up email inboxes.

Setting clear expectations and goals is the backbone of any remote operation. Without face-to-face supervision, remote teams thrive on clarity. Think of it like setting the GPS before a road trip. You define the deliverables, outline the timelines, and make sure everyone knows the destination. Regular performance assessments aren't just about checking boxes; they're about ensuring everyone's moving in the same direction. It's not micromanaging; it's guiding. This clarity helps manage workloads and keeps the team aligned with the company's objectives, ensuring that even when people are miles apart, they're still on the same page.

Building a sense of belonging in a remote setting might seem like a tall order. After all, how do you foster camaraderie when everyone's behind a screen? Virtual team-building exercises are a great start. Whether it's a trivia night, an online escape room, or just a casual chat about the latest Netflix binge, these activities break the ice and build connections. Celebrating milestones and achievements together is another way to unite the team. Did someone hit a sales target? Finish a big project? Shout it out to the whole team. These celebrations create a shared experience, reinforcing the idea that everyone is part of something bigger, even if they're working from a kitchen table or a corner café.

To keep things running smoothly, equip your team with the right tools and resources. Access to secure VPNs and cloud services ensures that everyone can work safely and efficiently from anywhere. It's like giving them a toolkit for success, no matter where they are. Offering stipends for home office setups can also make a big difference. It shows that you care about their work environment and are willing to invest in their comfort and productivity. A well-equipped home office isn't just about ergonomics; it's about creating a space where employees can thrive, free from the distractions that can plague remote work.

Managing remote teams is less about overseeing and more about facilitating. It's about creating an environment where team members feel connected, informed, and empowered to do their best work, no matter where they are. As you navigate this remote landscape, remember that the goal is to build a team that's as cohesive and effective as any in-house crew. With the right strategies, you can turn geographic distance into a mere footnote in your business story.

With a remote team running smoothly, it's time to turn our attention to the financial side of scaling. Up next, we'll explore how to manage your business finances effectively, ensuring every dollar supports your growth goals.

Chapter 5: Financial Management for Scaling

Picture this: You're at your favorite coffee shop, sipping a latte, and suddenly it hits you—you're not just savoring a drink, but thinking about the economics behind each frothy cup. There's rent, beans, barista salaries, and more. Just like that, you realize your business is a lot like this coffee shop, a complex blend of flavors that need just the right balance. And at the heart of it all? Cash flow. It's the lifeblood of any business, the espresso shot in your financial cappuccino. Without it, you're just left with a cup of hot milk. Let's dive into turning that cash flow into a steady stream, ready to fuel your scaling ambitions.

Understanding cash flow dynamics is crucial. It's not just about the money coming in and going out; it's about timing and cycles. Cash flow differs from profit. While profit is about the difference between revenue and expenses, cash flow focuses on when that money actually moves. Think of cash flow as the rhythm of your business, where timing is everything. Industries have their unique cycles. Retail might see a surge during holidays, while construction could peak in warmer months. Understanding these cycles helps you anticipate and plan for leaner times, ensuring your business doesn't run out of steam when you need it most.

Implementing cash flow management practices can feel like learning a new dance move. At first, it's awkward, but once you get the hang of it, you glide across the floor. Start with cash flow forecasting techniques. Forecasting is like peering into the financial future, letting you plan for upcoming expenses and income. It's your crystal ball, minus the mysticism. Accounts receivable and payable management is another crucial step. Keep track of who owes you money and who you owe. The goal is to speed up incoming payments and manage outgoing ones. Delaying supplier payments while accelerating customer payments can help maintain a positive cash flow, a strategy often used by savvy business owners.

Utilizing cash flow tools and software is like having a personal financial advisor who works around the clock. Platforms like QuickBooks and Xero offer powerful features to track and optimize cash flow. They provide real-time updates, helping you make informed decisions quickly. These tools are more than just fancy spreadsheets; they're dynamic systems that integrate seamlessly with your existing processes. They offer insights and analytics that can highlight trends and forecast needs, providing you with a comprehensive view of your financial health.

Maintaining positive cash flow requires some clever tactics. Negotiating better payment terms with suppliers can give you a buffer when cash is tight. It's all about building relationships and finding win-win scenarios. Short-term financing options can also be a lifesaver, bridging gaps when cash doesn't flow as smoothly as expected. Lines of credit or business credit cards can offer temporary relief, but use them wisely. You don't want to end up paying more in interest than you gain in liquidity.

Reflection Section: Cash Flow Check-Up

Take a moment to review your cash flow situation. Are there any patterns or cycles you hadn't noticed before? What steps can you take to improve your current cash flow management? Write down three specific actions you'll implement in the next month to enhance your cash flow.

Effectively managing cash flow is about staying ahead of the curve. It's like being the conductor of your business orchestra, ensuring every section plays in harmony. With the right tools and strategies, you can keep your business running smoothly, prepared for whatever financial challenges come your way.

Strategic Investment Planning

Picture yourself at a junction, making a choice about which route will lead your business to success and growth. Strategic investment planning acts as your navigation tool, guiding you through these decisions with clarity and assurance. The first step is to pinpoint valuable investment prospects. Consider it as searching for treasure, where market analysis serves as your digging tool. You must delve into industry movements, consumer preferences, and competitive environments. Is there an emerging technology that could transform your operations? Or maybe a niche market that's ready for exploration? Assessing the return on investment (ROI) is vital at this stage. It's similar to checking the forecast before heading out; you want to make sure your resources produce the best results. Weigh potential benefits against risks to confirm that your investments align with your business objectives.

Google's financial management strategy exemplifies the importance of scaling effectively through strategic reinvestment and foresight. In the early days, co-founders Larry Page and Sergey Brin, along with former CEO Eric Schmidt, employed a dual strategy: maximizing cash flow while pursuing ambitious investments in emerging technologies. Once Google achieved profitability with its innovative AdWords model, instead of becoming complacent, the leadership invested heavily in ground-breaking initiatives like the acquisition of Android and YouTube. This was not merely an act of diversification; it was a deliberate strategy to secure future revenue channels and lessen reliance on a single source of income.

Acquired in 2005, Android has since evolved into one of the most widely utilized mobile operating systems in the world. Likewise, the purchase of YouTube for $1.65 billion in 2006 proved to be a financial genius, generating billions in annual ad revenue today. These strategic investments demonstrated Google's capability to balance immediate profitability with a long-term vision, allowing the company to expand its operations while maintaining a robust financial standing. Their strategy illustrated that effective financial management encompasses more than just minimizing expenses or maximizing profits—it involves reinvesting in future endeavors to facilitate ongoing, exponential growth.

Diversification serves as your cushion in the uncertain investment landscape. It's like ensuring you don't place all your assets in a single venture. By balancing short-term and long-term investments, you can build a portfolio capable of withstanding any challenges. Short-term investments may enhance your cash flow and maintain smooth operations, while long-term investments, like technology or innovation, can prepare your business for upcoming successes. Adopting new technology can be transformative. Whether it involves automating operations or improving customer experiences, investing in innovation helps distinguish you from competitors. The essential point is to spread your investments across various sectors, reducing risk and boosting the likelihood of a favorable return.

Developing an investment strategy resembles creating a work of art. It takes vision, expertise, and a bit of imagination. Ensure your investments are in harmony with your business growth phases. Are you in the initial stages, concentrating on establishing a brand, or are you poised to expand into new territories? Each phase demands distinct strategies. Carry out a comprehensive risk evaluation to identify possible challenges. It's akin to checking your path for obstacles. Evaluating risks empowers you to make educated choices, ensuring your investments back your long-term aims. Formulate a strategy that ties ambition to practicality, crafting a blueprint that steers your investment decisions while keeping you on track.

Overseeing and fine-tuning investments is a continuous endeavor. It's like caring for a garden; you need to nurture what thrives and trim back what doesn't. Regular reviews of your investments enable you to monitor performance and implement necessary changes. Are your investments achieving their targets, or do they require adjustment? Set standards for divesting, such as poor performance or misalignment with objectives. This guarantees you don't invest further resources into ventures that no longer benefit you. Remain watchful and adaptable, prepared to shift when necessary, and always keep an eye on new possibilities.

Strategic investment planning revolves around making intelligent decisions that advance your business. With the correct strategy, you can establish a diverse portfolio that balances risk with reward, aligning with your vision and growth ambitions. As you delve into these prospects, remember that each choice shapes your business's future.

Exploring Loans and Funding Options

Imagine standing at the brink of a financial abyss, gazing into the vast expanse of business loans and funding opportunities. It's a chaotic realm, but understanding the landscape can be the key to either smooth scaling or struggling to stay afloat. Firstly, let's examine business loans. They are the foundation of conventional funding. Term loans and lines of credit are the two key players in this field. Term loans are straightforward: you receive a lump sum to be repaid over a fixed time with interest. It's similar to taking a mortgage for your business: predictable yet often needing collateral. Lines of credit, however, provide flexibility. They function more like credit cards, allowing you to borrow up to a limit and only pay interest on the amount you use. During times of low cash flow, these can be lifesavers, providing the space to handle unforeseen expenses. Additionally, there are Small Business Administration (SBA) loans—often viewed as the ultimate option for small businesses. They typically offer favorable terms and lower interest rates, but the qualifying criteria can be as challenging as earning a golden ticket to Willy Wonka's factory. A solid credit history, a robust business plan, and a bit of patience are essential to accessing these funds.

But what happens if traditional loans feel unsuitable? It's time to consider alternative funding avenues. Crowdfunding platforms like Kickstarter and Indiegogo have revolutionized the financing landscape. They enable you to present your business idea to a wide audience, gathering small contributions from numerous supporters. It's akin to having a multitude of friends support your dream. Angel investors and venture capitalists are another option, often searching for innovative ideas with considerable growth potential. These investors bring not just capital, but also valuable experience, mentorship, and connections. It's like catching a ride with a seasoned driver who knows all the shortcuts. Just remember, they typically want equity in return, so be prepared to share the pie.

Preparing for a loan application can feel like gearing up for a marathon. Creating a compelling business plan is your starting line. This plan isn't just a document; it's your business's story, outlining where you've been, where you're going, and how you plan to get there. Lenders want to see a clear path to success, with financial projections that show you're not just dreaming but planning. Strengthening your credit profile is another critical step. Pay down existing debts, resolve any discrepancies, and ensure your credit report shines like a freshly polished apple. Lenders are more likely to bet on you if your financial history shows responsibility and reliability.

Once you've secured funding, managing debt responsibly is paramount. It's like keeping your car in the right lane, avoiding unnecessary swerves and potential crashes. Start with a debt-to-equity ratio analysis. This helps you understand how much debt your business carries compared to its equity, giving you a clearer picture of your financial health. If you find the balance tipping too heavily toward debt, it might be time to consider refinancing options for better terms. Refinancing can reduce monthly payments or lower interest rates, freeing up cash for other needs. Just remember, refinancing isn't a get-out-of-jail-free card; it's a chance to reorganize and optimize your financial strategy.

Navigating loans and funding alternatives requires a blend of strategy, patience, and a dash of courage. It's about finding the right fit for your business's needs and ensuring every financial decision supports your growth goals. Whether you're courting traditional loans or exploring the world of alternative funding, the key is to stay informed and proactive.

Financial Forecasting for Future Growth

Ever found yourself daydreaming about winning the lottery, only to snap back to reality and realize that a solid plan is your best bet for future success? That's what financial forecasting is for your business—a plan, not a dream. It's the blueprint that anticipates financial needs and aligns them with your strategic goals. Picture financial forecasting as a roadmap through the wild terrain of entrepreneurship. Without it, you're just wandering aimlessly, hoping you'll stumble upon a pot of gold. Forecasting allows you to anticipate cash needs, identify potential shortfalls, and make informed decisions about where to invest or cut back. By aligning your financial goals with your overall business strategy, you ensure every dollar is spent with purpose and precision.

Creating accurate financial projections might sound like a task for the math wizards, but fear not—it's more approachable than you think. Start with historical data analysis. Look at your past performance, identifying trends and patterns. It's like being a detective, piecing together clues from your financial history to predict future outcomes. Scenario planning adds another layer of insight. Consider different growth paths your business might take, from the "steady as she goes" approach to the "rocket ship to the moon" trajectory. Each scenario comes with its own set of financial implications, helping you prepare for whatever the market throws your way. By planning for multiple possibilities, you're building flexibility into your forecasts, ensuring you're ready to pivot when needed.

Now, let's talk about the tools that make forecasting a breeze. Excel forecasting templates are a classic choice. They're like your trusty old car—reliable and familiar, but maybe lacking a few bells and whistles. For more advanced needs, specialized forecasting software steps into the spotlight. These tools offer real-time data, sophisticated financial modeling, and the ability to integrate with other systems you're already using. They're the futuristic sports car of financial planning, sleek and efficient. By leveraging technology, you gain insights that manual methods simply can't provide, allowing for more accurate and timely forecasts. The right tool can transform forecasting from a chore into a strategic advantage, giving you the confidence to make decisions with clarity.

But forecasting isn't a once-and-done deal. It requires regular review and adjustment. Think of it like tending to a garden. You can't plant seeds and walk away, expecting them to flourish without care. Quarterly forecast reviews keep your projections in line with reality, allowing for adjustments based on actual performance and market changes. Maybe a new competitor entered your space or a supply chain hiccup threw off your costs. Whatever the case, regular reviews help you adapt, ensuring your forecasts remain relevant and actionable. Adjusting forecasts based on these reviews is crucial. It's about being agile, responding to shifts with speed and accuracy. A static forecast is about as useful as a map without updates, leading you astray when the landscape changes.

Financial forecasting is your compass in the world of business. It provides direction, clarity, and the ability to navigate the complexities of growth with confidence. With accurate projections, appropriate tools, and regular adjustments, you're equipped to face the future head-on, ready to seize opportunities and tackle challenges with ease.

Cost Management in a Scaling Business

Running a business is a bit like juggling flaming torches. You're constantly trying to keep everything in the air without getting burned. As you scale, understanding your cost drivers helps you manage this juggle. Every business has its unique set of costs, but they generally fall into a couple of categories: direct vs. indirect costs and variable vs. fixed costs. Direct costs are those that are directly tied to the production of your goods or services—think raw materials and labor. Indirect costs, on the other hand, are a bit sneakier. They include things like rent and utilities, costs that keep the lights on but don't directly tie to a product. Then there are variable costs, which fluctuate with your level of production, and fixed costs, which remain constant regardless of output, like that landlord who expects rent even if the shop's empty. Recognizing these categories helps you identify where your money goes and where you might tighten the belt.

Once you've pinned down where your cash flows, it's time to trim the fat without losing the flavor. Enter cost reduction strategies. Lean management practices are all about efficiency, cutting out waste and focusing on what truly adds value. Picture a chef who knows exactly how to slice each ingredient to minimize waste and maximize taste. Lean management encourages a similar mindset. It's about streamlining processes, reducing redundancies, and ensuring that every step in your operation adds value. Strategic sourcing and procurement can also play a major role. By negotiating better deals with suppliers and exploring alternative sourcing options, you can reduce costs without compromising quality. It's like finding a new vendor who offers the same high-quality beans for your café at a fraction of the price.

Keeping an eye on business expenses is like managing a household budget. You track where every dollar goes, ensuring you're not spending more on takeout than groceries. Expense tracking tools and software can be invaluable allies here. They offer real-time visibility into spending, helping you spot trends and adjust as needed. Implementing budgetary controls adds another layer of discipline, setting limits on different expense categories to ensure you stay within your financial means. It's like putting a cap on your monthly coffee shop visits— tough love, but necessary for financial health.

Balancing cost management with growth initiatives is where the real magic happens. You want to grow, but you also don't want to end up in the red. Conducting a cost-benefit analysis for growth initiatives helps you weigh the potential returns against the expenses. It's about making informed decisions and ensuring your investments support your scaling ambitions without draining your resources. Prioritizing high-impact cost reductions can also free up funds for growth. Focus on areas where cuts won't compromise quality or customer satisfaction. It's like finding ways to save on packaging without sacrificing the unboxing experience for your customers.

Cost management is about making smart, strategic decisions that support your business goals. By understanding your cost drivers, implementing effective reduction strategies, and balancing expenses with growth, you can create a lean, efficient operation that's prepared to thrive as you scale.

With a solid handle on costs, you're ready to look at the broader picture: creating a robust company culture that supports your growth and engages your team. This balance between financial discipline and cultural investment is key to sustainable success.

In the late 1990s, Amazon was starting to build momentum as an online bookstore. Founder Jeff Bezos envisioned broadening the company's scope beyond just books to create an "everything store," but scaling up presented significant challenges in cost management. During those initial years, Amazon was losing substantial amounts of money in its quest for growth. The company had to grow quickly while being mindful of its spending.

One of the most notable cost management tactics that Bezos implemented was a culture of frugality. Rather than investing in expensive office furniture or extravagant perks, Amazon employees used desks crafted from repurposed doors. The message was clear: every dollar spent should be warranted and directly support the company's mission. This frugal attitude infiltrated all tiers of the business and became integral to Amazon's core values. The emphasis on cost efficiency enabled Amazon to reinvest the savings into innovations and enhancements in customer service, facilitating its quick scaling without falling into financial traps.

This strict cost-control culture did not stifle growth; it fueled it. By staying resourceful and reinvesting wisely, Amazon was able to broaden its range of offerings, improve its operations, and ultimately transform into one of the most valuable companies globally.

The takeaway for small business owners is evident: as you expand, keep a steadfast focus on efficient cost management. Growth does not have to be accompanied by excessive expenses. Embracing a disciplined spending strategy, where every dollar aligns with your broader goals, can differentiate between unsustainable expansion and lasting success. To conclude this chapter, remember: it's not merely about becoming larger; it's about growing wisely, always keeping an eye on your financial health.

Make a Difference with Your Review!

"The best way to find yourself is to lose yourself in the service of others." – Mahatma Gandhi

Would you do a simple act to help someone else who might be struggling to scale or grow their small business just like you start their journey to scaling their small business?

Our mission is simple: making small business scaling clear and achievable for everyone. But we need your support. Reviews are what guide others to books like this one, helping them make life-changing decisions.

Leaving a review takes less than a minute but could inspire...

...another small business that will make a difference

...another entrepreneur to build a secure future

...another family to gain financial freedom

...another dream to come true

Ready to make that difference? Simply scan this QR code which will take you directly to the review page:

Your kindness makes all the difference!

Your biggest fan, Nathaniel Mathew

Chapter 6:
Marketing and Brand Building

Imagine walking into a cafe and the barista knows your name, your order, and even asks about your dog, Max. This connection makes you feel special like you're part of a community. That's the magic of a strong brand story. It's not just about what you sell but the experience and emotions you create. Crafting a compelling brand story can transform your business from just another name into a beloved staple in your customers' lives. It's the narrative that tells people who you are, why you exist, and why they should care. It's about creating a relationship, not just a transaction.

In the world of business, a clear and consistent brand message is your north star. It guides every decision, from how you answer the phone to the design of your website. Your unique selling propositions (USPs) are the heart of this message. They're what set you apart from the competition. Maybe it's your commitment to sustainability or your lightning-fast delivery service. Whatever it is, make it clear. Your mission and vision are equally crucial. They're the why behind your what. Perhaps you aim to revolutionize the tech industry or simply make the best darn cupcakes around. Articulate this vision so your audience knows exactly what you stand for. It's like giving them a window into your soul, showing them the passion and purpose driving your business.

Creating a narrative that connects emotionally with customers is where the magic happens. It's like telling the story of your brand through the eyes of a hero—your customer. Consider the storytelling technique of the hero's journey. Your customer is the hero, facing challenges and seeking solutions. Your brand steps in as the guide, helping them overcome obstacles and achieve their goals. This approach makes your story relatable and memorable. Incorporate customer testimonials and success stories to add depth and authenticity. These real-world examples show that you've helped others, building trust and credibility. It's like having your customers sing your praises, creating a chorus of positive experiences that attract new followers.

Consistency is key in brand storytelling. Imagine if your favorite novel changed its plot halfway through. Confusing, right? Your brand story should be seamlessly integrated across all channels. Align website content with social media messaging to create a unified voice. This consistency extends to marketing collateral, ensuring everything from business cards to email signatures reflects your brand's essence. It's about creating a harmonious experience, where every touchpoint reinforces your message. This alignment helps customers recognize and remember your brand, building familiarity and trust.

Take a look at LEGO, a company that skillfully reinvented itself by forging a strong emotional bond with its customers. In the early 2000s, LEGO struggled with falling sales and was on the verge of financial disaster due to excessive expansion and a lack of focus in its product offerings. The pivotal moment came when the company embraced its legacy and re-centered its brand on storytelling and engaging fans. They introduced interactive campaigns and produced content that struck a chord, including the popular film The LEGO Movie in 2014. This film served not only as entertainment but also as a two-hour advertisement that rekindled passion for the brand across different generations and increased sales by almost 15% that year.

LEGO also took advantage of social media and user-generated content, prompting fans to showcase their own creations and stories. The "LEGO Ideas" platform permitted enthusiasts to propose their designs, with successful entries being turned into actual products. This strategy not only boosted customer loyalty but also involved fans in the brand's growth. LEGO's approach of cultivating a community-focused brand turned it into a cherished name with enduring appeal, illustrating how genuine storytelling and customer participation can elevate a brand's visibility and profitability.

As your business evolves, so should your brand story. It's like a living document that reflects your growth and adaptation. Update your narrative with new milestones—maybe you've expanded into new markets or launched an innovative product line. Reflect on feedback and market changes, showing that you're responsive and in tune with your audience. This adaptability keeps your story fresh and relevant, ensuring it resonates with current and future customers.

Reflection Section: Your Brand Story

Take a moment to jot down your brand's core message, mission, and vision. What are your USPs? How do they set you apart? Think about your narrative—what's the emotional journey you want to take your customers on? Consider how you can integrate this story across all channels to maintain consistency and build a strong, memorable brand.

In the end, a compelling brand story is more than just words on a page. It's the heart and soul of your business, connecting you with your audience on a deeper level. With a clear message, an emotional narrative, and consistent storytelling, you can transform your brand into a trusted and beloved entity in your customers' lives.

Leveraging Social Media for Brand Awareness

Navigating social media can resemble the challenge of locating your car in a vast parking lot. With numerous platforms, each featuring unique characteristics, figuring out where to start can be intimidating. However, it is essential to choose the right platforms for your target audience. It's similar to picking the ideal location for a party—you want to be where your guests gather. Begin by conducting a demographic analysis. Who is your target customer? Are they young people taking selfies on Snapchat or business professionals browsing LinkedIn? Once you identify your audience, you can evaluate engagement metrics to discover where they are most active. Perhaps Instagram serves as their preferred source for visual inspiration, or they turn to Twitter for quick updates. Aligning your social media strategy with these insights guarantees you're not merely shouting into the void but rather engaging with those most likely to purchase what you offer.

Producing content that people are eager to share is akin to crafting a message in a bottle—you want it to travel widely and reach new destinations. The key is to create material that is engaging and relatable. Visual storytelling via Instagram Stories can be an effective strategy. Use images, videos, and behind-the-scenes insights to develop a narrative that captivates your audience. This platform is ideal for sharing experiences that make your brand feel more like a friend than an impersonal corporation. On Facebook, interactive polls and quizzes can ignite conversation and encourage sharing. People enjoy voicing their opinions, especially in a light and entertaining manner. By integrating these features, you transform passive viewers into active participants, enhancing the reach and impact of your content.

Now, let's discuss finances and how to use them wisely in social media advertising. Paid social media can boost your brand's visibility like a megaphone at a bustling concert. The secret lies in creating targeted advertising campaigns. Think of it as a sniper approach instead of using a shotgun. Leverage the data you've collected about your audience to craft ads that resonate directly with their interests.

A/B testing your ad creatives is also crucial for optimizing your marketing efforts. Consider it like trying on different outfits to see which one makes the best impression—it involves testing various elements of a hook, body, and call to action (CTA) on the same video or image to learn what appeals most to your audience. By experimenting with different headlines, videos, and CTAs, you can gather data on which combinations attract attention and boost engagement. This ongoing process entails running two or more versions of an ad simultaneously to compare their performance against key metrics, such as click-through rates, conversion rates, or customer acquisition cost. Over time, these tests yield valuable insights into which components work best for your target audience, allowing you to make informed adjustments. The ultimate objective is to refine your strategy so your ad spending is more efficient, maximizing return on investment (ROI) and ensuring your marketing budget is utilized effectively. This prevents the frustration of creating and promoting multiple unique videos that fail to perform, instead of keeping the same video while testing different variations to discover a successful formula. By creating one video, along with four hooks, two bodies, and two CTAs, you'll wind up with 16 video variations. This approach seems far simpler and more efficient than producing 16 entirely unique videos. It enables you to identify what works, which you can then apply to future advertising campaigns, allowing for quicker results and cost savings.

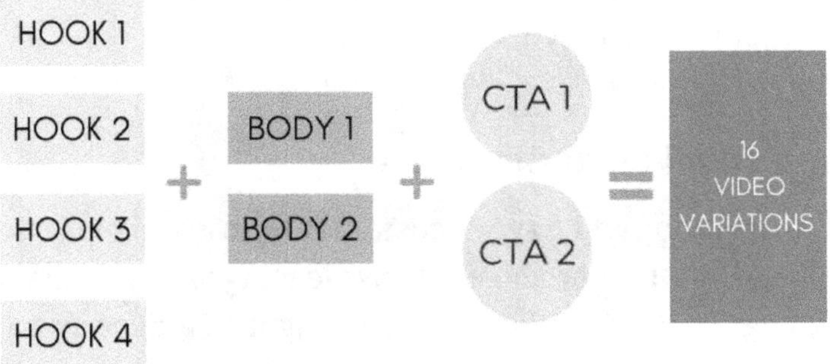

Regular A/B testing keeps you nimble, helps you adapt to trends, and consistently enhances the effectiveness of your advertising strategies.

Engagement is the essence of social media. Simply posting content and walking away isn't sufficient; you need to nurture those interactions like a gardener caring for plants. Keep an eye on and promptly respond to comments and messages. This demonstrates to your followers that you're not merely a brand but a lively entity that values their opinions. Imagine the effect of a swift reply or a thank-you to a loyal customer. These small acts foster a sense of community and loyalty. Engaging with user-generated content presents another strong tactic. When customers share photos or stories about your product, it's as though they are marketing for you. Acknowledge these contributions, share them on your own channels, and observe as your community becomes even stronger.

Social media is a constantly shifting environment, brimming with opportunities to connect and engage with your audience in significant ways. By selecting the appropriate platforms, creating compelling content, using advertising effectively, and building community through interaction, you can enhance your brand's visibility and establish enduring relationships with your customers.

Building a Loyal Customer Base

Imagine a scenario: you have a customer who strolls into your store every week, come rain or shine, always leaving with a smile and a full shopping bag. That's the ideal situation, right? Cultivating a loyal customer base is similar to forming a group of friends who eagerly anticipate seeing you. One effective way to foster this loyalty is through customer loyalty programs. These programs are like a secret handshake between you and your customers, turning casual shoppers into devoted patrons. Points-based reward systems are a popular choice. Each purchase earns points, which can be redeemed for discounts or freebies. It's like a mini treasure hunt where every transaction brings your customer closer to a reward. Another tactic is offering exclusive access to new products or special events for your loyal customers. Imagine hosting a VIP night where your best customers get a sneak peek of a new line or a tasting of your latest menu. These gestures make your customers feel appreciated and valued, reinforcing their loyalty.

Now, let's talk about the cornerstone of customer loyalty: exceptional customer service. It's the warm smile that greets your customers, the friendly chat that makes them feel at home, and the extra mile you go to ensure their satisfaction. Personalized customer interactions can turn a one-time buyer into a lifelong fan. It's about remembering their name, their usual order, or that they recently mentioned a big life event. These small touches create a personal connection that goes beyond the transaction. And when issues arise—and they will—resolving them swiftly and effectively is key. Treat every complaint as an opportunity to shine, to show your customers that they matter to you. A quick, empathetic response can turn a negative experience into a positive one, leaving the customer more loyal than before.

Building a community around your brand is another strategy that pays dividends. It's like hosting a neighborhood block party where everyone feels welcome and connected. Start by creating spaces where your customers can interact with each other and with you. Brand-specific forums or groups, whether online or in-person, provide a platform for sharing experiences, asking questions, and building relationships. Organize community events and meetups that align with your brand's values and mission. These gatherings don't have to be extravagant; even a casual coffee morning or a workshop can bring people together. The goal is to foster a sense of belonging, making your brand not just a business but a community hub.

And, of course, listening to your customers is crucial. Soliciting and acting on customer feedback isn't just good practice; it's a powerful tool for growth. Customer satisfaction surveys are a straightforward way to gather insights. Ask the right questions and be open to the answers, even if they're not what you want to hear. This feedback is like a compass, guiding you toward improvements and innovations that resonate with your audience. But gathering feedback is only half the battle. Implementing changes based on customer suggestions shows that you value their input and are committed to continuous improvement. It's like having a conversation where both sides are heard and respected, strengthening the bond between you and your customers.

Coca-Cola's timeless marketing campaigns highlight the power of brand building and customer connection. The "Share a Coke" campaign, launched in 2011, replaced the brand's logo on bottles with common first names and phrases like "Bestie" and "Family." This personalized marketing strategy encouraged customers to seek out bottles with their own names or those of friends and family, turning a simple beverage purchase into a social experience. The campaign exploded in popularity, driving a significant increase in sales and brand loyalty. By focusing on creating a personal and memorable experience, Coca-Cola reinforced its reputation as more than a drink—it's a shared moment. This approach underscores how marketing that taps into emotional and social connection can turn a brand into an essential part of people's lives.

Content Marketing for Small Businesses

Let's talk about content marketing, the unsung hero of small business growth. Imagine it as your trusty sidekick, always there to help you connect with your audience and spread your message far and wide. But, like any good sidekick, it needs a plan. Developing a content strategy that aligns with your business goals is crucial. Start by identifying what your audience craves. Are they hungry for how-to guides, craving interviews with industry experts, or perhaps they just want a good laugh with some light-hearted content? Knowing their needs helps you tailor your content, making it relevant and engaging. Next, map this content to the customer journey. Think of it as a road trip. You need to know where your customers are starting from and where they want to go. Are they just discovering your brand or are they ready to make a purchase? Tailor your content to guide them along this path, offering the right information at the right time.

Once you've got your strategy, it's time to shake things up with various content formats. Gone are the days when a simple blog post would suffice. Today, you need a buffet of content types to keep your audience engaged. Blog posts and articles are fantastic for sharing in-depth knowledge and establishing your expertise. They're like the bread and butter of content marketing. But don't stop there. Podcasts and webinars offer a dynamic way to connect with your audience. They provide a platform for storytelling, sharing insights, and even hosting interviews with industry leaders. These formats are perfect for those moments when your audience is multitasking—driving, exercising, or even doing the dishes. By offering a mix of content types, you cater to different preferences, keeping your audience engaged and coming back for more.

Now, let's get into the nitty-gritty of SEO, the magic ingredient that increases your content's visibility and draws organic traffic to your website. Keyword research is where the magic begins. It's like mining for gold in the digital world, uncovering the words and phrases your audience uses to find products and services like yours. Implement these keywords strategically in your content to boost your search engine rankings. But don't overstuff them; Google has a keen nose for that trick. On-page SEO techniques are also crucial. This includes optimizing meta tags, headers, and images to ensure your content is easily discoverable. It's like dressing up your content for the search engine ball, making sure it's presentable and ready to impress.

Measuring content performance and ROI is where you separate the wheat from the chaff. It's not just about feeling good because you've ticked the content box. You need to know what's working and what's not. Analyzing website analytics is your best friend here. Dive into traffic sources to see where your visitors are coming from. Are they finding you through search engines, social media, or perhaps a well-placed guest post? Tracking lead generation and conversion rates helps you understand how effective your content is at turning curious visitors into loyal customers. These metrics provide invaluable insights, guiding your content strategy and helping you make informed decisions about where to focus your efforts.

Content marketing is a powerful tool for small businesses, offering the chance to connect, engage, and convert your audience in meaningful ways. With a solid strategy, diverse formats, and a focus on SEO, you can ensure your content not only reaches but resonates with your target audience.

Implementing Data-Driven Marketing Strategies

In today's fast-paced business environment, leveraging customer data isn't just a nice-to-have; it's your secret weapon for crafting targeted marketing strategies. When you analyze purchasing behavior, you're essentially peeking behind the curtain into what makes your customers tick. Maybe you notice a trend where your products fly off the shelves during the holiday season, or perhaps there's a spike every payday. Recognizing these patterns allows you to tailor your marketing efforts to align with these buying habits. Segmenting audiences based on demographics and behavior is like having a personalized roadmap for each group. One audience might respond well to a flashy social media campaign, while another prefers in-depth email newsletters. By understanding who your customers are and how they behave, you can ensure your marketing messages hit the right note every time.

Having the right tools at your disposal can make all the difference in optimizing your marketing strategies. Google Analytics is a powerhouse when it comes to understanding website traffic. It's like having a magnifying glass that lets you see where visitors are coming from, what pages they linger on, and where they decide to jump ship. These insights can inform everything from content tweaks to full-blown redesigns. Similarly, CRM systems track customer interactions across various touchpoints. Imagine being able to pull up a customer's history with a click, understanding their past purchases, preferences, and any previous issues. This information is invaluable for crafting personalized marketing efforts that speak directly to individual customer needs.

Personalization is no longer optional. It's expected. Customers want to feel seen and understood, not like another cog in the marketing machine. Personalized email marketing campaigns are a fantastic way to deliver this tailored experience. Instead of a generic "Dear Customer" greeting, you can address them by name, recommend products based on past purchases, and even send birthday discounts. Tailored product recommendations can make customers feel like you're reading their mind. By using data to predict what they might like, you're not just selling them a product; you're offering a solution to a problem they didn't know they had. This level of personalization fosters deeper connections and builds loyalty.

Marketing isn't a set-it-and-forget-it endeavor. It's a constant cycle of testing, learning, and refining. A/B testing marketing messages is like running a science experiment. You send out two versions of an email or ad and see which performs better. Maybe one headline grabs attention, while another falls flat. By analyzing the results, you can make informed decisions about which direction to take. Similarly, continually refining audience targeting based on campaign results ensures you're not wasting resources on ineffective strategies. It's about being nimble, ready to pivot and adapt as new data comes in.

Embracing these data-driven strategies allows you to create marketing campaigns that are not only effective but also meaningful. They enable you to connect with your customers on a deeper level, providing them with the value and experience they crave. As you continue to refine and optimize these efforts, remember that the world of marketing is always evolving. Stay curious, stay informed, and never stop experimenting. Your customers—and your bottom line—will thank you for it.

As we wrap up this chapter, remember that data-driven marketing is your compass in navigating the ever-changing business landscape. It empowers you to make smarter decisions, build stronger relationships, and drive growth in ways that resonate with your audience. Up next, we'll explore how to balance growth and quality, ensuring your business not only expands but also excels in delivering value.

Chapter 7:
Balancing Growth and Quality

Imagine you're at a bustling farmer's market. You're surrounded by vendors selling everything from fresh honey to handmade jams. But one stall catches your eye. The vendor's goods are meticulously arranged, each jar of jam is labeled with care, and somehow, each sample tastes even better than it looks. It's clear this vendor has gone above and beyond in maintaining quality. Now, imagine your business as that stall. You want your products or services to stand out not just for their appeal but for the consistent quality that keeps customers coming back. This chapter is about setting those high standards and maintaining them as your business grows. It's about ensuring that as you scale, quality doesn't just keep up but leads the way.

Let's start by defining quality benchmarks. Think of these as the yardstick by which you measure everything your business produces, from the tangible products to the customer interactions that define your brand. Establishing clear, measurable benchmarks is crucial. They align with your business objectives, ensuring that every facet of your operations meets the standards you've set. When it comes to product performance, quality metrics might include durability, efficiency, or customer satisfaction scores. For service interactions, consider metrics like response time, resolution efficiency, and overall customer satisfaction. These benchmarks serve as your guiding light, ensuring that everyone in your organization understands what's expected and consistently delivers.

Incorporating industry best practices is another step toward elevating quality. These are tried-and-tested methods proven to work across your industry. Consider ISO certification processes. While they might sound like something only big corporations need, they offer a structured approach to quality management that benefits businesses of all sizes. It's like having a blueprint for success, providing a clear framework for maintaining standards. Benchmarking against competitors is another effective strategy. According to Quality Digest, competitive benchmarking often results in a 20% productivity improvement. By comparing your operations to those of your direct competitors, you gain insights into what works well and where you might improve. It's not about copying but learning and adapting, ensuring your business stays ahead of the curve.

Your quality standards should also align with your brand promise. This is the essence of what your business stands for. It's the promise you make to your customers, and ensuring your quality benchmarks reflect this promise is paramount. Consider hosting brand promise alignment workshops. These sessions bring your team together to discuss and define what quality means in the context of your brand. It's about ensuring everyone is on the same page and committed to delivering on that promise. Your customers chose you for a reason, and maintaining that trust is key to sustaining growth.

Regularly reviewing and updating your standards is essential to keep pace with evolving customer expectations and industry advancements. Annual quality review meetings provide a platform for assessing current benchmarks and identifying areas for improvement. They're your opportunity to reflect on what's working and what might need a tweak. As technology evolves, incorporating advancements into your standards ensures you're not left behind. It's about being proactive, not reactive, and continually pushing the boundaries of what quality means for your business.

Reflection Section: Define Your Quality Standards

Take a moment to jot down your current quality benchmarks. Consider both product performance and customer service interactions. Are they aligned with your business objectives? What industry best practices could you incorporate to elevate your standards? Reflect on how these benchmarks align with your brand promise and identify areas for potential improvement.

Setting and maintaining quality standards is about creating a culture of excellence within your business. It's about ensuring that as you grow, your commitment to quality remains unwavering. With clear benchmarks, industry best practices, and a focus on continuous improvement, you're well on your way to not just meeting but exceeding customer expectations.

Quality Control Processes for Scaling

Consider constructing a house of cards. It requires careful balance, precision, and patience. Now, picture doing this while the cards are being delivered to you at double the speed. That's the experience of scaling a business without effective quality control measures in place. As you expand, preserving quality turns into a juggling challenge. Total Quality Management (TQM) and Six Sigma methods can serve as your guiding principles, assisting you in establishing strong systems that adapt to higher production and service needs. TQM focuses on embedding quality in every aspect of your business. It's a comprehensive approach that emphasizes ongoing improvement and customer satisfaction. On the other hand, Six Sigma is your best strategy for reducing defects and variability. It's akin to having a disciplined coach ensuring you perform your best at all times.

Technology significantly enhances quality control efforts. Imagine a team of robots carefully inspecting each product for faults before it departs the factory. Automated inspection systems accomplish just that, guaranteeing every item meets standards without missing a beat. They are like having a legion of perfectionists ensuring no mistakes slip through, averting costly issues. Quality management software solutions are equally vital. These tools assist in monitoring and managing quality throughout your organization, providing insights and analytics that influence your decisions. They function like a dashboardthat reveals the health of your operations in real-time, pinpointing areas needing attention and celebrating those that excel.

However, having the right technology is insufficient on its own. The right personnel are needed to ensure everything functions smoothly. Enter cross-functional quality teams. These groups comprise diverse talents, each contributing their expertise. Think of them as your quality task force, supervising different functions and guaranteeing everything aligns with your standards. Collaboration tools facilitate teamwork among these groups by breaking down barriers and enhancing communication. Regular interdisciplinary quality review sessions are essential. They resemble team huddles, ensuring everyone is aligned and striving toward the same objectives. These sessions allow members to share insights, address challenges, and develop strategies for improvement.

Gathering and analyzing quality data is fundamental to any effective quality control system. It's about understanding what works well and what requires adjustments. Statistical process control charts are invaluable in this process. They act as your quality barometer, displaying trends and fluctuations in your processes. Real-time quality dashboards elevate this further by providing immediate insights to inform your decisions. They serve as your eyes and ears, offering a clear view of your operations and spotlighting areas for enhancement. By utilizing this data, you can make informed decisions that promote quality improvements and support your growth initiatives.

Envision operating a bakery where every loaf of bread is flawlessly baked, each cookie perfectly shaped. Expanding without sacrificing quality is akin to achieving this perfection on a larger scale. It involves establishing systems that grow and adapt alongside you, ensuring every product or service you provide meets your high standards. With the appropriate processes in place, you can concentrate on what you excel at—delighting customers and growing your business without losing sight of quality.

Customer Feedback as a Quality Tool

Picture yourself managing a small café, and a customer enters, orders a latte, and exits looking dissatisfied. You're left questioning whether it was too hot, too cold, or perhaps just not to their liking? Grasping customer feedback is like obtaining the answers to these puzzles without guessing. Establishing channels to receive feedback is crucial for staying attuned to your customers' thoughts and feelings. Begin with online feedback forms. These are simple to create and can be integrated into emails or your website. They provide a convenient way for customers to express their opinions whenever they like, whether praising your new pastry or suggesting improvements. A customer feedback hotline is another excellent option. At times, people prefer talking to a real person. A dedicated line for customers to share their views can deliver immediate insights and foster stronger connections. It's like having an open-door policy, inviting customers to voice their thoughts whenever they wish.

During the early 2000s, as Microsoft expanded its software offerings, it faced criticism regarding quality issues with Windows Vista. Gates and his team promptly shifted focus to ensure that the subsequent release, Windows 7, rectified previous grievances. They employed thorough beta testing and feedback mechanisms to enhance user experience. The result was a successful product, demonstrating the importance of balancing growth with quality.

Once you've gathered this treasure trove of feedback, the next step is analyzing it for actionable insights. It's akin to sorting through a pile of stones to discover the diamonds. Utilize sentiment analysis of customer reviews to gauge the overall mood and sentiments regarding your products or services. Are customers predominantly satisfied, or is there a common frustration lurking beneath the surface? Classifying feedback based on product features can also yield clarity. If numerous reviews mention that your latte art needs enhancement, it's a clear indication that this area requires attention. By dissecting feedback into specific components, you can better target areas for improvement. Incorporating this feedback into quality improvement plans is where the magic happens. It's not just about listening but acting on what you hear. Feedback-driven product iterations allow you to tweak and refine your offerings based on real customer input. Consider establishing customer advisory boards. These groups, made up of your most loyal customers, can provide invaluable insights and help guide product development. They're like having a built-in focus group that genuinely cares about your brand's success. By involving customers in the process, you not only improve your products but also create a sense of ownership and loyalty among your customer base.

Communicating changes based on feedback is the final piece of the puzzle. Customers want to know that their voices matter and that their input leads to real change. Consider sending out customer newsletters highlighting the updates and improvements made thanks to their feedback. It's like saying, "Hey, we heard you, and here's what we did." Publicly acknowledging feedback on social media is another powerful way to show appreciation. Share a post thanking customers for their suggestions and detailing how you've implemented their ideas. This transparency not only builds trust but also encourages others to share their thoughts, knowing they'll be valued and heard.

Exercise: Feedback Channel Assessment

Take a moment to review your current feedback channels. Are they easy for customers to access? Are you receiving enough feedback to inform meaningful changes? Identify one new method of gathering feedback you could implement and plan how you'll analyze and act on the insights you receive.

Embracing customer feedback as a tool for quality improvement is about more than just collecting data. It's about building a dialogue with the very people who keep your business running and using their insights to drive continuous improvement. By creating effective channels for feedback, analyzing it carefully, integrating it into your plans, and communicating changes, you create a cycle of growth and enhancement that benefits both your business and your customers.

Training for Consistency

Picture this: you're at a restaurant where every dish is perfectly cooked, every time. No matter who's in the kitchen, the results are always top-notch. That consistency doesn't happen by accident. It's the result of robust training programs that ensure every staff member knows exactly what to do and how to do it. In business, this kind of reliable quality starts with comprehensive training programs. Think of onboarding quality training modules as your new hires' first taste of what your business stands for. They set the stage for everything that follows, ensuring every employee starts on the right foot. You want those first days to be not just informative but inspiring, laying a foundation that supports your brand's values and objectives.

But training isn't a one-time event—it's a continuous journey. The world changes fast, and your team needs the skills to keep up. Continuous learning and development resources are vital. They're like a well-stocked library, offering knowledge and tools that empower employees to grow and adapt. Whether it's through online courses, workshops, or industry conferences, these resources ensure your team is always learning and always improving. They keep everyone sharp and ready to tackle new challenges with confidence. Over time, this ongoing education fosters a culture where growth and innovation flourish, benefiting both your team and your business.

Uniformity in training materials and practices is crucial to maintaining that golden consistency. Think of it like a symphony orchestra, where every musician follows the same sheet music. Standard operating procedures (SOP) manuals are your business's sheet music, providing clear, step-by-step instructions for every process. Video tutorials add an interactive element, offering visual guidance that makes learning engaging and effective. Together, these tools ensure every employee receives the same information in the same way, reducing errors and enhancing efficiency. Consistent training materials are like a universal language, creating a cohesive environment where everyone is on the same page.

Evaluating the effectiveness of your training programs is as important as the training itself. It's like checking the rearview mirror while driving—essential for staying on course. Regular assessments help you gauge whether your training meets quality objectives and identify areas for improvement. Training feedback surveys provide insights from those on the receiving end, revealing what's working and what's not. Performance evaluations post-training offer a tangible measure of success, highlighting how well employees apply what they've learned. This ongoing assessment ensures your training remains relevant and impactful, adapting to meet the ever-evolving needs of your business and its people.

Promoting a culture of continuous learning transforms a workplace into a vibrant ecosystem of growth and innovation. Just as a garden thrives with sunlight and water, employees flourish when they're encouraged to learn and develop. Offer incentives for skill development—maybe it's a bonus for completing a course or recognition for new certifications. Access to online learning platforms makes acquiring new skills easy and accessible, breaking down barriers to education. When learning becomes part of your company's DNA, everyone benefits. Employees feel valued and empowered, ready to contribute their best to the team. This dynamic environment drives engagement, satisfaction, and retention, setting your business up for long-term success.

Balancing Speed and Excellence

In the fast-paced world of business, the constant struggle to balance speed with quality can feel like trying to ride a unicycle while juggling flaming torches. You have to keep everything in motion, ensuring that nothing gets dropped. Prioritizing tasks based on impact is your safety net in this balancing act. Picture an impact versus effort matrix, a simple yet powerful tool that helps you evaluate which tasks will provide the biggest bang for your buck. By mapping out tasks according to their potential impact and the effort required, you can zero in on high-impact quality initiatives that drive growth without compromising on excellence. It's like picking the ripest fruits from the tree, focusing your energy where it counts most.

Adopting agile practices is another strategy to ensure you're moving swiftly without leaving quality behind. Agile methodologies, originally designed for software development, have proven effective across industries. They encourage quick iteration and adaptability, allowing you to respond to changes and challenges with agility. Think of agile sprint planning as a series of short, focused bursts of activity where teams aim to complete specific tasks. This approach keeps projects dynamic and responsive rather than bogged down by endless planning. Regular retrospectives are the secret sauce here, offering a chance to reflect on what went well and what didn't. It's like pressing pause to review the game plan, ensuring continuous improvement and alignment with quality goals.

Implementing a rapid prototyping approach allows you to test and refine products quickly, without losing sight of quality. Rapid prototyping is like sketching a rough draft before painting a masterpiece. It enables you to create minimum viable products (MVPs) that capture the essence of your idea without overcommitting resources. By releasing these MVPs to a select audience, you can gather valuable feedback early on, using it to refine and perfect the final product. Feedback loops are critical in this process, offering insights that guide iterations and improvements. It's a bit like testing a new recipe on friends before unveiling it at a big dinner party—fine-tuning based on real reactions.

Managing resources effectively is the key to supporting both rapid growth and quality assurance. Resource allocation strategies help you distribute time, money, and manpower where they're needed most. It's about ensuring you have the right people and tools in place to maintain quality while scaling up. Balancing short-term wins with long-term quality goals is an art. You want to achieve quick victories that boost morale and momentum, but not at the expense of your long-term vision. It's a bit like running a marathon, where pacing is everything. You need to keep moving forward, but with a strategy that ensures you don't burn out before crossing the finish line.

As we wrap up this chapter, think of balancing speed and excellence as the secret to sustainable growth. It's about making smart choices, adapting quickly, and never letting quality fall by the wayside. With these strategies in place, you're not just moving fast—you're moving with purpose and precision. And as you navigate this delicate balance, remember that each decision shapes the future of your business.

Chapter 8:
Creating a Strong Company Culture

Picture this: Your business is like a family reunion, where every member gets along, knows their role, and brings something special to the table. They share laughs, support each other, and work together seamlessly. It sounds idyllic, right? But let's be honest, most of us have experienced the chaos of a family gathering where Uncle Bob's jokes fall flat and Cousin Alice insists on bringing her questionable potato salad. The key to transforming your business from a chaotic picnic into a harmonious feast is creating a strong company culture. It all starts with defining and living by your core values.

Defining your company's core values is like setting the GPS for your business journey. They're the fundamental beliefs that guide your decisions and behavior, providing a common direction for everyone involved. But how do you figure out what those values should be? Start by gathering your team for a workshop dedicated to brainstorming what truly matters to your business. Encourage open dialogue and creativity, ensuring everyone's voice is heard. You might be surprised to discover that the intern values teamwork just as much as the CEO values innovation. Remember, it's not a one-person show; it's about reaching a consensus that resonates with the entire team. Leadership input is crucial here, but it should guide rather than dictate the process. Once you've identified these core values, they should feel authentic and specific—like a custom-tailored suit that fits your business perfectly.

Communicating these values clearly to all stakeholders is vital. It's not enough to slap them on a poster in the break room and call it a day. They need to be woven into the fabric of your company, making them an integral part of your daily operations. Start by incorporating them into your onboarding materials. This ensures new hires understand what the company stands for from day one. Regular discussions at team meetings can keep these values top of mind. It's like watering a plant—you need consistent care and attention to see it flourish. Use these meetings as a platform to reinforce how these values drive decision-making and influence the workplace culture.

Once your core values are defined, it's time to embed them into everyday actions. This is where the rubber meets the road, transforming lofty ideals into tangible behaviors. Encourage values-based decision-making throughout the organization. When faced with a challenge, ask how your core values can guide the resolution. It might be choosing honesty over saving face or prioritizing quality over speed. Recognition programs aligned with these values can further reinforce their importance. Celebrate team members who exemplify your values, whether through a monthly award or a simple shoutout in a team meeting. Recognizing these behaviors encourages others to follow suit, creating a ripple effect that strengthens the entire culture.

Zappos' culture under Tony Hsieh was ground-breaking. From the very beginning, Hsieh highlighted the significance of company culture as the foundation of the organization. He believed that satisfied employees would result in pleased customers, prompting Zappos to invest significantly in creating an environment that honored individuality, enjoyment, and a collective sense of mission. New employees underwent extensive cultural training, with the company even offering $2,000 for those who wished to resign if they felt misaligned with its principles. This daring strategy ensured that only those who were genuinely committed remained, cultivating a cohesive and enthusiastic team. The results were substantial: Zappos not only gained recognition for its outstanding customer service but also developed a loyal workforce that propelled the company's impressive growth. This approach proved that a robust culture is more than just perks; it involves instilling values that resonate throughout the organization.

But values aren't static; they should evolve as your business grows and changes. Just like you wouldn't wear the same clothes you did a decade ago, your values should adapt to fit the current landscape. Schedule annual value review sessions to assess how well they align with your business objectives and the realities of the market. Gather feedback from employees to gain insights into what's working and what needs adjustment. This process is like tuning an instrument, ensuring your values stay in harmony with your company's goals and the needs of your team.

Reflection Section: Aligning Values with Action

Take a moment to consider the values of your company. Are they explicitly stated, effectively communicated, and incorporated into everyday practices? Think about organizing a workshop with your team to assess their relevance and significance. Foster open discussions and collaboration to ensure the values resonate with everyone involved.

By proactively defining, sharing, and embodying your core values, you establish a company culture that operates smoothly, where everyone understands their role and collaborates toward shared objectives. This sturdy foundation not only enhances employee satisfaction and engagement but also attracts individuals who align with your mission. As your business expands and evolves, make sure to frequently evaluate and adjust your values to keep them in line with your vision and the ever-shifting business environment.

Building an Innovative Culture

Envision your business as a garden. Each plant symbolizes an idea, and with the right environment, they can flourish into something remarkable. To nurture this garden, it's vital to promote creative thinking among your team. It's akin to providing them with a blank canvas and a set of colors, encouraging them to create freely, without fear of criticism. Innovation workshops can be an excellent way to initiate this process. These workshops serve as venues where bold ideas are not merely accepted—they're celebrated. Inspire your team to think unconventionally, challenge conventional wisdom, and delve into 'what if' scenarios that are often overlooked. It's less about pinpointing the right solution and more about exploring all the possibilities.

Regular brainstorming sessions should be an essential part of your schedule. Imagine a room populated by individuals unafraid to express their wildest ideas. The guideline? No criticism allowed. It functions like a play area for adults, where participants can bounce from one concept to another, building on each other's ideas. The real magic occurs when unexpected relationships arise, leading to innovations that nobody anticipated. Encourage contributions from all levels of the organization, from interns to executives, as you never know where the next significant idea might originate. The focus is to create a supportive environment where everyone feels safe to share their ideas, no matter how unconventional they may be.

After stimulating creativity, it's time to allocate the necessary resources to turn those ideas into reality. Consider it as watering your garden to ensure those seeds of innovation can grow and thrive. Dedicating resources to innovation is essential, not optional. Think about establishing innovation labs or designated areas where your team can explore without interruptions. These spaces ought to be outfitted with the latest tools and technologies, providing everything necessary to test and refine concepts. It's akin to giving your team a sandbox where they can build, deconstruct, and reconstruct without any fear of failure.

Budgets for exploratory projects are also vital. They act like fertilizer that accelerates the growth of ideas. By reserving funds specifically for innovation, you clearly indicate that creativity is not only welcomed but expected. These budgets need not be extensive, but they should be substantial enough to offer promising ideas a fair chance. Urge your team to present their ideas and justify the funding. This process not only sharpens their pitching abilities but also fosters a sense of ownership and accountability for their initiatives.

Acknowledging and rewarding innovative attempts is the final component of the equation. It's like giving your team recognition and saying, "Great job, continue this momentum!" Innovation awards or acknowledgment can inspire employees to keep pushing their limits. Celebrate these accomplishments publicly, whether through company newsletters or social media highlights, to motivate others to think creatively. Public recognition is impactful; it not only lifts spirits but also sets a standard for others to aspire to. It cultivates a culture where innovation transcends mere jargon and becomes a lifestyle.

Establishing a risk-taking environment is crucial for nurturing innovation. It's about reassuring your team that experiencing failure is acceptable—as long as they learn from it. Encourage calculated risks, where the potential benefits justify the risk. It's similar to teaching a child to ride a bike; they might fall several times, but each fall serves as a lesson in balance. Likewise, learning from failures without fearing repercussions is essential. It fosters resilience and nurtures a mindset where setbacks are perceived as opportunities for growth.

By developing a culture of innovation, you are not just promoting creativity; you are ingraining it into the core of your business. It involves creating an atmosphere where ideas can thrive, resources are accessible for their cultivation, and recognition fuels the aspiration to continually challenge boundaries.

Employee Engagement Strategies

Picture yourself addressing your team, a collective with varied backgrounds, skills, and aspirations. They are not merely employees; they embody the essential spirit of your organization. And let's be real, keeping them engaged isn't just a nice-to-have—it's crucial for the success of your business. So, how do you create an environment where people feel excited to come to work every day? One way is by developing meaningful engagement programs that resonate with your team. These initiatives go beyond the usual perks and delve into what truly matters to your employees. Consider launching wellness initiatives that promote physical and mental health. It could be in the form of yoga classes, meditation sessions, or even an office smoothie bar. These small gestures show your team that you care about their well-being, not just their output.

Professional development opportunities are another fantastic way to keep your team engaged. We all want to grow and improve, and your employees are no different. Offering access to workshops, online courses, or even mentorship programs can make a huge difference. It's like equipping them with a toolkit for success, helping them sharpen their skills and climb the career ladder. Not only does this foster a sense of loyalty, but it also enhances your team's capabilities, benefiting your business in the long run.

Listening to your employees is a powerful tool for engagement. Imagine having an anonymous suggestion box where your team can freely share their thoughts and ideas without fear of judgment. This approach encourages openness and honesty, providing valuable insights into what's working and what could be improved. Regular engagement surveys can also be instrumental in gauging employee satisfaction and identifying areas for development. It's like taking the pulse of your organization, helping you understand the mood and needs of your team. By actively seeking and acting on feedback, you demonstrate that their opinions matter, which can significantly boost morale and engagement.

Creating a sense of belonging is another cornerstone of employee engagement. People want to feel like they're part of something bigger than themselves, a community where they're valued and appreciated. Consider organizing team-building activities that foster camaraderie and connection. Whether it's a company retreat, a friendly sports match, or a virtual game night, these events can help break down barriers and build strong relationships. Celebrating individual and team achievements is equally important. Acknowledging hard work and accomplishments with small tokens of appreciation, like personalized notes or shout-outs during meetings, can make employees feel seen and appreciated.

Aligning engagement strategies with employee aspirations is crucial. Everyone has career goals and dreams, and as a leader, it's important to support and nurture those ambitions. Personalized career development plans can provide a clear path for growth, helping employees understand how they can achieve their goals within your organization. One-on-one career counseling sessions offer a safe space for open discussions about aspirations and challenges. These conversations can uncover hidden talents and aspirations, allowing you to tailor development opportunities to individual needs. It's like helping someone find the right trail on a hike, guiding them toward a rewarding future.

As you implement these engagement strategies, remember that the goal is to create a work environment that feels like a second home, where employees are motivated, fulfilled, and excited to contribute. It's about building a culture where engagement is not just a buzzword, but a lived experience that drives your team forward. Each step you take to enhance engagement is an investment in your people, your culture, and ultimately, your business's success.

Aligning Culture with Business Goals

Aligning your company culture with your business goals is like aligning the wheels of a car: when they're in sync, the ride is smooth, and you reach your destination faster. But when they're out of alignment, you're in for a bumpy drive that can derail your progress. Your company's culture should resonate with your strategic objectives, creating a cohesive environment where everyone's rowing in the same direction. This requires more than just good intentions; it demands a structured approach, starting with culture audits. Think of these as regular check-ups that assess how well your culture supports your business goals. You'll look at various aspects, like employee satisfaction and alignment with core values, to see where you stand. It's a bit like visiting the doctor—not always fun, but necessary to catch issues before they snowball. By integrating cultural goals into your strategic planning, you ensure that culture isn't an afterthought but a driving force behind your business strategy.

Communicating the connection between culture and business success is crucial. It's one thing to have a strong culture, but if no one understands its impact on the company's success, it might as well be invisible. Leadership plays a pivotal role here. When leaders articulate how the company culture contributes to business achievements, it creates a narrative that everyone can get behind. Use leadership presentations to highlight cultural impacts, sharing stories and insights that illustrate how a positive culture has driven success. Imagine a company-wide newsletter that celebrates cultural achievements, shining a spotlight on those who embody the company's values. It's like throwing a party for your culture, where everyone gets to see the value of their contributions.

The work doesn't stop there. Continuous monitoring and adjustment of cultural initiatives are essential to keep up with the ever-changing business landscape. Regular reviews of cultural Key Performance Indicators (KPIs) help you track progress and identify areas for improvement. These KPIs could measure employee engagement, customer satisfaction, or innovation rates—whatever aligns with your business goals. It's like having a dashboard that shows how well your culture is performing. And remember, adaptability is key. Markets evolve, and your culture should, too. Be ready to pivot and tweak your initiatives to stay relevant and effective. This adaptability ensures your culture remains a strong pillar supporting your strategic objectives, rather than a relic of the past.

Engaging leadership in cultural promotion is the final step in aligning culture with business goals. Leaders set the tone for the entire organization, and their actions speak louder than words. When leaders model the desired culture, it sends a powerful message that can inspire and motivate employees. Leadership training focused on cultural influence can equip leaders with the tools they need to promote a positive culture effectively. Think of it as giving them a megaphone to amplify the company's cultural values. Visible participation in cultural activities, whether it's attending team-building events or leading by example in daily interactions, reinforces the importance of culture. It's like seeing the captain of a ship actively steering and navigating, rather than just giving orders from afar.

As you work to align your culture with your business goals, remember that this is an ongoing process. It requires dedication, open communication, and a willingness to adapt. When done right, it creates a harmonious environment where culture and strategy work hand in hand, propelling your business toward success. As you move forward, keep these principles in mind to ensure your company culture supports your strategic objectives and fosters an environment where everyone thrives.

Chapter 9:
Exit Strategies and Long-term Planning

Imagine you're a chef, and your restaurant is your masterpiece. It's bustling, the kitchen's in full swing, and the tables are filled. But every great chef knows there comes a time to hang up the apron. Maybe you're dreaming of that villa in Tuscany or just want to focus on your next big adventure. Whatever the reason, having an exit strategy is like having a secret recipe—it's essential for ensuring your hard work doesn't go up in smoke.

Planning Your Exit Strategy

Navigating the realm of exit strategies can resemble selecting the right dish at a buffet—exciting but a bit overwhelming. Each alternative presents its distinct advantages and disadvantages. Selling to a competitor or a strategic buyer can provide a swift and profitable exit, delivering liquidity but often at the expense of giving up control. You may end up observing from a distance as someone else takes charge. On the other hand, a Management Buyout (MBO) enables your trusted team to assume control, allowing you to gradually withdraw while maintaining the business in familiar hands. This option can be an excellent way to ensure continuity and preserve the values you've established over the years.

Then there's the captivating appeal of an Initial Public Offering (IPO). Going public resembles stepping onto a red carpet—it's glamorous and can yield substantial rewards, yet the journey is laden with obstacles and uncertainties. It necessitates thorough preparation and a readiness to disclose your financial details to the public. For those in a family business, succession planning may be the ideal route. Passing the leadership to the next generation can be profoundly fulfilling, but it demands meticulous planning to prevent the issues of unprepared heirs and family conflict. Ensuring your successors are prepared to lead is just as essential as choosing the right successor from the beginning.

The timing of your exit is just as important as selecting the right strategy. It's akin to determining the perfect moment to take that soufflé out of the oven. Too early, and it's undercooked; too late, and it may collapse. Analyzing market conditions is vital. Pay attention to economic indicators and industry trends. Are interest rates favorable? Is your sector experiencing growth? Selling during a boom can enhance your value, while a downturn might mean accepting less. Being aware of these trends can guide you in making a wise decision, ensuring you maximize your hard-earned investment.

Getting your business ready for sale is comparable to preparing a house for an open house. You want everything to shine in order to attract potential buyers. Streamlining processes and finances is a good starting point—think of it as tidying up your garage. Make sure your records are flawless and your operations efficient. Strengthening customer relationships is equally crucial. A devoted customer base serves as a form of curb appeal, attracting interested buyers. When potential buyers see a strong, loyal following, they are more likely to invest in your business's future.

Effective communication is the essential ingredient that binds everything together. When formulating your exit plan, it's vital to engage your stakeholders. Your employees, investors, and partners deserve to know what lies ahead. Informing your team about the exit strategy can avert rumors and drops in morale. It's similar to sharing the kitchen timetable with staff—everyone understands their responsibilities and expectations. Address their concerns openly, assuring them of their job security. Investors and partners also need to be kept informed. Engaging them early can help ensure alignment and support during the transition.

Exercise: Formulate Your Exit Strategy

Grab a pen and paper, or open your preferred note-taking application, and write down your thoughts on each exit option. Reflect on your personal objectives, the condition of your business, and the market environment. Which strategy best aligns with your vision? List the advantages and disadvantages of each to clarify your direction. This exercise is about initiating a dialogue with yourself, not about making a final choice today.

Creating an exit strategy is a crucial component of your business journey. It's about ensuring your legacy persists and that you depart on your terms. By grasping your options, timing your move wisely, preparing your business meticulously, and communicating effectively with your stakeholders, you lay the groundwork for a successful transition. Whether you're handing over control or selling to the highest bidder, a well-planned strategy can significantly impact the outcome.

Assessing Your Business's Worth for Sale

Let's be honest—determining the value of your business can feel like trying to appraise your grandmother's treasured jewelry. You recognize its worth, but how do you assign a numerical value? Thankfully, there are a few reliable methods to achieve this. The first is the asset-based valuation method. This approach is fairly straightforward. You calculate all your business assets, such as cash, equipment, and property, and subtract any liabilities. Think of it as clearing out the garage and selling everything except the hidden issues. This method is most effective for businesses with considerable tangible assets or those preparing to liquidate. However, it doesn't take into account potential future earnings or intangible assets like your brand's reputation or that secret sauce recipe you've perfected over the years.

Following that, there are the earnings multiple methods, which involve multiplying your company's yearly earnings by a factor that corresponds to industry standards. Picture your earnings as the main ingredient in a recipe, and the multiple as the seasoning that adds flavor. This method is favored because it considers the business's capacity to generate profits in the future. It's like betting on a racehorse that's consistently performed well. The challenge lies in selecting the correct multiple, which can vary based on market conditions, industry trends, and even your business's unique attributes.

The discounted cash flow (DCF) analysis is another tool in the valuation toolkit. It's like peering into a crystal ball to predict future cash flows and then applying a discount rate to determine their present value. Picture your future earnings as a stream of income, flowing steadily over time. DCF analysis helps calculate what that stream is worth today. It's particularly useful for businesses with predictable cash flows, but it requires some serious number-crunching and assumptions about future growth, interest rates, and market risks.

Now that you've got a handle on valuation methods, let's talk about boosting your business's value before sale. Improving profit margins is a great place to start. Imagine your business is a pie, and profit margins are the slices you get to keep. The bigger the slice, the more enticing your business becomes to potential buyers. Consider reviewing your pricing strategies, cutting unnecessary costs, and optimizing processes to maximize efficiency. It's like trimming the excess fat to reveal a leaner, more attractive business. Diversifying revenue streams is another way to add appeal. Relying on a single source of income is like putting all your eggs in one basket. By expanding your offerings or tapping into new markets, you create stability and growth potential, which buyers love to see.

When it comes to valuing your business, getting a second opinion can be invaluable. Engaging professional valuation experts is like hiring a seasoned mechanic to inspect a used car before buying. Business appraisers have the experience to assess your company's worth accurately, and financial advisors specializing in mergers and acquisitions can provide insights tailored to your exit strategy. They bring objectivity to the process, helping you avoid overvaluing sentimental aspects or undervaluing hidden gems. These experts can also guide you through the complexities of valuation methods and ensure you present a compelling case to potential buyers.

Gathering essential documentation for valuation is like preparing your house for sale. You want everything in tip-top shape to impress potential buyers. Start with audited financial statements, which provide a clear picture of your business's financial health. These documents are your business's resume, showcasing its strengths and achievements. A comprehensive business plan and growth projections are equally important. They highlight your company's vision, market position, and future opportunities. Think of them as the blueprint for your business's potential, enticing buyers with the promise of what's to come.

Your business is more than just numbers on a balance sheet. It's a story of hard work, dedication, and dreams realized. By understanding valuation methods, enhancing your business's value, engaging professional expertise, and preparing thorough documentation, you set the stage for a successful sale. Each step is an opportunity to showcase the full potential of what you've built, ensuring you receive the recognition and reward you deserve.

Transitioning Leadership

Picture this: You're at the helm of a thriving business, the captain of your ship. But even the best captains know when it's time to pass the wheel to a new leader. The key to a smooth transition lies in identifying and developing successors who can steer the ship with confidence. Think of it as planting seeds for the future—selecting potential leaders who will grow and thrive with the right support. Leadership training programs are like the rich soil, providing the nutrients necessary for growth. They offer structured learning, covering everything from decision-making to conflict resolution. It's about equipping future leaders with the tools they need to navigate the complex waters of business leadership.

Mentorship opportunities within your organization are equally vital. Imagine them as the sunlight that helps these seeds grow. Pairing emerging leaders with experienced mentors fosters a culture of learning and support. It's like having a coach on the sidelines, ready to guide them through challenges and celebrate their victories. This relationship not only builds confidence but also creates a pipeline of talent, ensuring your business remains in capable hands long after you've stepped down.

Now, onto the nuts and bolts—creating a transition plan. This isn't the time for winging it. A well-thought-out plan is your roadmap, ensuring a seamless handover. Start by setting a timeline for transition activities. Think of it as a countdown clock, ticking down to the big day. Outline each step, from announcing the transition to the final handover. This timeline keeps everyone on track and minimizes surprises. Clearly define the roles and responsibilities of outgoing and incoming leaders. It's like a relay race, where the baton must be passed smoothly. Both parties need to know what's expected of them and when, to avoid any missteps.

Maintaining business continuity during leadership changes is crucial. Consider interim leadership arrangements to bridge any gaps. It's like having a safety net, ensuring operations continue without a hitch. Communication plans are your best ally here. Keep internal and external stakeholders informed every step of the way. Picture this as a transparency window, allowing everyone to see what's happening and why. Open dialogue builds trust and alleviates concerns, keeping morale high and rumors at bay.

But let's not forget the human side of leadership transitions. Addressing the emotional and cultural aspects is just as important as the practical ones. Support programs for staff during changes can make all the difference. Think of them as a comforting hand on the shoulder, reassuring your team that everything will be okay. Whether it's counseling services or team-building activities, these programs provide the support needed to navigate the emotional rollercoaster of change. Preserving company culture through transitions is another critical aspect. Your culture is the heart and soul of your business, and it must be protected. Encourage new leaders to embrace and uphold these values, ensuring they remain the guiding principles for the company's future.

Leadership transitions are like passing a treasured family recipe down to the next generation. It takes careful planning, nurturing, and a dash of patience. By identifying and developing successors, creating a detailed transition plan, maintaining business continuity, and addressing emotional and cultural aspects, you set the stage for a successful handover. It's about ensuring your business continues to thrive, even as you step back and watch from the sidelines, knowing you've left it in good hands.

Long-term Vision for a Sustainable Business

Building a lasting business is a bit like planting a tree. You need to think long-term, nurturing it so that it grows strong and withstands the test of time. Developing a strategic long-term plan is your roadmap to sustainable growth beyond any exit strategy. Start by identifying those big-picture goals that go beyond just making money. What do you want your business to achieve in five, ten, or even twenty years? It might be expanding into new markets, innovating your product line, or becoming a leader in your industry. These goals are your north star, guiding every decision and strategy. Strategic initiatives are the stepping stones towards these goals. They might involve investing in research and development, adopting new technologies, or forming strategic partnerships. Think of them as the actionable steps that keep you moving forward, ensuring your business remains relevant and competitive.

Now, let's talk sustainability. It's not just a buzzword; it's a crucial component of modern business strategy. Integrating environmental and social sustainability into your model isn't just good for the planet—it's good for business. Customers today are more informed and conscientious, often choosing brands that align with their values. Implementing eco-friendly practices can range from reducing waste and energy consumption to sourcing materials responsibly. Consider it a way to future-proof your business, as regulations and consumer preferences increasingly favor sustainable practices. Corporate social responsibility (CSR) initiatives are another avenue to explore. These programs reflect your commitment to positive social impact, whether through community engagement, ethical labor practices, or charitable giving. They enhance your brand's reputation and build trust with stakeholders, demonstrating that you're not just about profits but also about making a difference.

Businesses that thrive in the long run are those that can adapt to changing market conditions. It's like surfing; you need to be agile, ready to pivot when the waves shift. Continuous market research and trend analysis are your tools for staying ahead. They help you understand the evolving landscape, anticipate challenges, and seize new opportunities. Flexibility in business strategies allows you to respond swiftly to these changes. Maybe it means tweaking your product offerings, adjusting your marketing strategies, or even rethinking your business model. Being open to change is crucial. It's about having the courage to try new things and the wisdom to know when to let go of what no longer works.

Creating a culture of continuous improvement is like having a well-oiled machine that runs smoothly and efficiently. Encourage innovation at all levels of your business. This doesn't mean only the top executives get to make decisions. Empower your team to bring ideas to the table, fostering an environment where creativity thrives. Regularly review and refine your processes. It's not about fixing what's broken; it's about making what's good even better. This could involve streamlining operations, adopting new technologies, or enhancing customer service. By embedding a mindset of growth and development into your company culture, you create a workforce that is engaged and motivated to excel.

Reflection Section: Building a Sustainable Future

Take some time to brainstorm ideas for integrating sustainability into your business model. Consider your current practices and identify areas for improvement. Are there eco-friendly initiatives you can implement? What social impact can your business make in the community? Write down your thoughts and create a list of actionable steps to incorporate these ideas into your long-term strategy. This is your opportunity to align your business goals with broader societal values, ensuring a positive impact on the world around you.

Creating a long-term vision for a sustainable business is about more than just planning for the future. It's about building a foundation that supports growth, embraces change, and contributes positively to society. By developing a strategic plan, focusing on sustainability, adapting to market dynamics, and fostering continuous improvement, you set your business on a path to enduring success. As you look to the future, remember that the decisions you make today will shape the legacy you leave behind. So dream big, act wisely, and lead with purpose.

Chapter 10:
Case Studies - Learning from The Failures Of Big Brands

Have you ever thought about why certain companies thrive while others fail miserably? In this section, we'll thoroughly investigate actual case studies, learning from the blunders of prominent businesses that overlooked critical scaling principles. By analyzing these cautionary narratives, we'll reveal how these companies could have circumvented expensive errors—and how you can apply these insights to enhance your success. Prepare to uncover not only what succeeded but also what fell short, and how you can avoid encountering the same traps. We'll examine how their disregard for these 9 scaling principles led to notable losses and missed chances.

Snapchat's Journey Through Monetization Challenges

Snapchat's initial rise to fame was driven by a distinctive user experience that attracted millions, particularly from younger age groups. However, the company encountered a challenge when it failed to establish a solid financial management strategy. Early monetization attempts were restricted to basic advertisements and in-app purchases, proving inadequate for maintaining profitability as competitors devised more sophisticated revenue approaches. Snapchat's delayed shift towards utilizing augmented reality filters and interactive advertising solutions helped stabilize its income but came after valuable time and growth potential were squandered. The key lesson here is evident: a robust financial strategy must be integrated into the scaling process from the beginning. Without aligning rapid user growth with dependable revenue sources, businesses risk expanding towards financial instability and lost opportunities.

eBay's Mistakes in Global Expansion

eBay's swift transition to a global marketplace in the late 1990s provided a harsh lesson about the importance of understanding local markets. While the company excelled in the U.S., it misjudged cultural differences and user behaviors in new territories, particularly in Japan, where Yahoo! Auctions quickly surpassed it. eBay's inability to localize its business model and cater to the specific preferences of Japanese consumers resulted in its expansion efforts being undermined by regional rivals. This underscores a vital principle: global scaling necessitates comprehensive market research and the ability to adapt products or services. Small business owners should recognize that strategies effective in one region may not work elsewhere, and ignoring this understanding can lead to wasted resources and potential harm to their reputation.

Starbucks' Dilemma Between Quality and Speed

The early 2000s marked a period of aggressive growth for Starbucks, which opened six to seven locations daily around the world. However, this rapid expansion came with consequences: a decline in the brand's valued quality and customer experience. The intense growth led to service inconsistencies and diluted the intimate, community-oriented atmosphere that had been a key part of Starbucks' charm. Founder Howard Schultz took the courageous decision to temporarily close 7,000 stores to retrain baristas and concentrate on quality. The lesson here is that scaling should not compromise the essential elements that define a brand's identity. Small business owners must understand that growth should be careful and measured to uphold quality, ultimately ensuring long-term sustainability and customer loyalty.

Kodak's Reluctance to Adapt to Digital Innovation

Kodak's decline serves as a stark reminder of the dangers of overlooking technological progress. Even after inventing the first digital camera in 1975, Kodak opted not to pursue this innovation, fearing it would threaten their lucrative film business. As digital photography grew in popularity, Kodak found itself falling behind more nimble competitors that quickly embraced emerging technologies. The result was a dramatic fall from industry leader to near obscurity. For small business owners, this narrative highlights that harnessing technology and responding to market changes are crucial for successful scaling. Maintaining a rigid adherence to outdated models can result in missing the very momentum that drives others forward.

Blockbuster's Opportunity Lost with Netflix

Blockbuster's reluctance to change serves as a significant cautionary tale. At its height, Blockbuster dominated the video rental industry, operating thousands of stores worldwide. When Netflix proposed a partnership to Blockbuster in 2000, suggesting to handle the online rental service, Blockbuster's executives rejected the idea, convinced that their physical store model would keep them afloat. This narrow-mindedness proved disastrous. As streaming technology became more popular, Blockbuster struggled to compete against Netflix's more contemporary, customer-focused strategy. The important takeaway here is that growth necessitates flexibility. Small business owners should take heed: neglecting to adopt new business models and understand customer preferences can swiftly make even the most established businesses irrelevant.

Airbnb's Early Trust Challenges

Airbnb's initial experience highlights the necessity of addressing trust issues for successful growth. At first, the idea of letting strangers rent personal living spaces met significant doubt. Users were reluctant to reserve accommodations due to concerns about safety and quality. This trust deficit negatively affected the company's growth and revenue. By 2011, Airbnb was finding it tough to convert interested visitors into paying customers, significantly restricting their growth potential.

To navigate these challenges, Airbnb's founders took crucial steps that transformed their business. First, they invested in professional photography for their hosts, ensuring that listings featured appealing, high-quality images. This improvement instantly enhanced the perceived value and reliability of the platform. Furthermore, Airbnb launched the $1 million Host Guarantee program to safeguard hosts against property damage. These actions were strategic rather than merely cosmetic; they directly addressed users' primary concerns.

The outcomes were remarkable. After implementing these changes, Airbnb's bookings increased dramatically. The company's revenue in 2010 was merely $200,000, but by 2012, it skyrocketed to over $100 million—a remarkable leap. The initiatives aimed at building trust significantly contributed to this rapid growth, demonstrating how prioritizing user confidence can lead to substantial financial returns. By dismantling major trust hurdles, Airbnb not only improved its platform but also established a groundwork for explosive growth, ultimately becoming a multi-billion-dollar enterprise. This illustrates to small business owners that trust-building is crucial, and investing in user experience can transform an innovative idea into a market leader.

WeWork's Reckless Growth

WeWork's steep decline serves as a warning about the risks of rapid growth without a solid business model. Under Adam Neumann's leadership, WeWork grew internationally at an astonishing rate, supported by large funding and driven by ambitious, even extravagant, visions. However, the company lacked a definitive route to profitability. Elevated operating expenses and an excessive focus on expansion without strategic financial oversight led to a failed IPO and a significant drop in its valuation. For small business owners, this narrative is a vital reminder that growth requires financial responsibility and clear profit strategies. Chasing expansion at all costs can lead to overreach and the potential downfall of the business.

BlackBerry's Stagnation in Innovation

Once a leader in mobile technology, BlackBerry's decline from prominence illustrates the risks of complacency. At its peak, BlackBerry was a household name in business communication. Nonetheless, the company's inability to foresee the rise of touchscreen technology and the app-driven ecosystem led by Apple and Google sealed its demise. By the time BlackBerry attempted to adapt, it had already surrendered its market position to rivals that recognized the shifting landscape. This error teaches small businesses that ongoing innovation and attentiveness to market trends are essential for scaling. Growth without evolution results in being surpassed by more agile competitors.

These instances highlight that while scaling can elevate a business to remarkable heights, it must be undertaken with strategic understanding. Overlooking fundamental principles—be it financial management, technological adoption, adaptability, or quality maintenance—can turn growth potential into cautionary examples. For small business owners, deriving lessons from these narratives is crucial for establishing a route to sustainable success.Learning from these failures is crucial. It's about recognizing the red flags and making changes before it's too late. Successful businesses understand the importance of adapting, whether it's through careful market research, robust financial management, listening to customer feedback, or embracing technology. It's about building a foundation that supports growth without losing sight of what makes the business unique. In the next chapter, we'll explore how these lessons can be applied to create a sustainable business model that thrives in today's dynamic market.

Conclusion

So, here we are at the end of our journey together through the world of scaling small businesses. You've been with me every step of the way, unraveling the secrets of turning your business into a thriving, seven-figure success story. Let's take a moment to reflect on the core principles we've explored.

First and foremost, the nine scaling principles are your trusty compass. From bootstrapping to innovative financing, these principles are your roadmap. They guide you through the often tricky terrain of business growth. We've seen how major brands used these principles to rise from humble beginnings to market leaders as well as some case studies of others' who failed to apply these principles to their business resulting in major regrets and missed opportunities. Remember, it's about leveraging what you have, reinvesting wisely, and never underestimating the power of persistence.

A scalable operating system is your foundation. It's like the engine of your car, powering you through the ups and downs of scaling. We've talked about the importance of efficient workflows, the magic of automation, and the necessity of feedback loops. These elements keep your business running smoothly, so you can focus on what really matters—growth.

Speaking of growth, the case studies we've examined offer a treasure trove of lessons. Each story provided insights you can apply to your own journey. The key takeaway? Be adaptable and ready to learn from others' successes and missteps.

Let's not forget the financial strategies we've discussed. Optimizing cash flow, making strategic investments, and exploring funding alternatives are essential. These techniques ensure your business has the financial muscle to support its ambitions. As you expand, keeping a close eye on your finances is critical for sustained growth.

Building and managing effective teams is another cornerstone of success. Attracting top talent, fostering a supportive culture, and developing future leaders are vital. Your team is your greatest asset. They're the ones who will help turn your vision into reality.

Technology and automation are your allies in this journey. They make your business more efficient and scalable. Whether it's AI-driven customer support or automation tools, embracing technology can save time and boost productivity. It's about working smarter, not harder.

A strong company culture is the glue that holds everything together. Encouraging innovation, embracing diversity, and ensuring alignment with your goals are key. A positive culture attracts top talent and keeps them engaged and motivated.

On the marketing front, storytelling and brand-building are your secret weapons. Crafting a compelling narrative, engaging on social media, and using data-driven marketing strategies drive growth. Your brand is your story, and it's how you connect with your customers.

Balancing growth with quality is a delicate dance. You must maintain high standards while scaling. It's about listening to feedback, implementing robust quality controls, and never losing sight of what makes your product or service great.

For those facing limited capital, creative financing solutions and strategic partnerships are lifelines. They offer viable paths to scale without breaking the bank. Remember, it's not always about how much money you have but how creatively you use it.

As we look towards the future, exit strategies and long-term planning are crucial. Whether you're considering selling, transitioning leadership, or planning for sustainability, having a clear plan ensures you leave a lasting legacy.

Before we part ways, here are some key takeaways. Embrace those nine principles. Build a scalable operating system. Learn from others.

Manage your finances wisely. Foster a strong team and culture. Leverage technology. Tell your brand story. Balance growth with quality. Get creative with financing. Plan for the future.

Now, it's your turn. I encourage you to take these insights and run with them. Implement the strategies we've discussed. Use this book as your guide to transform your business. Start today. Even small changes can lead to big transformations.

And remember, the journey doesn't end here. Keep learning, keep adapting. Stay open to new ideas and innovations. The business world is ever-changing, and the most successful entrepreneurs are those who evolve with it.

I'm confident in your ability to succeed. You've got the tools, the insights, and the roadmap. Now, it's time to scale your business to new heights. Go forth and make your business the success story you've always envisioned. I'm cheering you on every step of the way.

Help a Fellow Business Owner?

Now that you've learned everything you need to scale your small business, it's your turn to share the journey and help others find the guidance they need.

By leaving your honest review on Amazon, you'll help other small business owners discover the tools to grow their dreams and keep the spirit of scaling alive.

Thank you for playing a vital role in passing this knowledge forward and helping us keep the momentum going.

Ready to make that difference? Simply scan this QR code which will take you directly to the review page:

Your biggest fan, Nathaniel Mathew

References

- *Bootstrapping: How to Bootstrap Your Startup* https://carta.com/learn/startups/fundraising/bootstrapping/

- *Alternative Lending For Small Business* https://www.bankrate.com/loans/small-business/alternative-lending/

- *Building Success Together: The Power Of Strategic ...*https://www.forbes.com/councils/forbesbusinesscouncil/2024/03/15/building-success-together-the-power-of-strategic-partnerships-in-business/

- *10 Best Crowdfunding Sites and Platforms in 2024* https://www.shopify.com/blog/crowdfunding-sites

- *Building Scalable Business Models* https://sloanreview.mit.edu/article/building-scalable-business-models/

- *Best Project Management Software Of 2024* https://www.forbes.com/advisor/business/software/best-project-management-software/

- *Agile: Taking Your Small Business To The Next Level* https://www.forbes.com/sites/tomtaulli/2021/08/02/agile-taking-your-small-business-to-the-next-level/

- *Building a Scalable IT Infrastructure for Your Startup* https://www.linkedin.com/pulse/building-scalable-infrastructure-your-startup-cloudactive-labs-shd0c?trk=public_post

- *Top Tech Stacks That Reigned Supreme In 2023* https://fullscale.io/blog/top-tech-stacks-reigned-supreme-in-2023

- *20 AI Tools To Supercharge Your Business And Productivity* https://www.forbes.com/sites/jodiecook/2023/09/11/20-ai-tools-to-supercharge-your-business-and-productivity/

- *10 Best Small Business Automation Tools for 2023* https://www.ventureharbour.com/10-small-business-automation-tools-to-save-time-increase-profit/

- *Strengthen your cybersecurity | U.S. Small Business ...* https://www.sba.gov/business-guide/manage-your-business/strengthen-your-cybersecurity

- *101 Employer Branding Strategy Ideas for 2023* https://www.themartec.com/employer-branding-brandwagon/101-employer-branding-strategy-ideas-for-2023

- *The Benefits of Outsourcing for Small Businesses* https://www.uschamber.com/co/start/strategy/benefits-of-outsourcing-small-businesses

- *Managing Remote Teams: 28 Tips and Best Practices in ...*https://www.digitalocean.com/resources/articles/managing-remote-teams

- *Hiring on a Budget: 10 Tips for Cash-Strapped Startups* https://www.recruiter.com/recruiting/hiring-on-a-budget-10-tips-for-cash-strapped-startups/

- *10 Best Practices to Manage Small Businesses Cash Flow* https://www.americanexpress.com/en-us/business/resources/grow-business/small-business-cash-flow-management/

- *Cash Flow Forecast Planning Software for SMBs in 2023* https://www.abacum.io/blog/best-cash-flow-forecasting-software-for-smbs

- *Beyond Banks: Alternative Funding for Startups* https://www.thehartford.com/business-insurance/strategy/alternative-funding-startup

- *How to use strategic financial planning and ... - Drivetrain* https://www.drivetrain.ai/post/strategic-financial-planning-strategic-financial-management

- *How to Tell a Compelling Brand Story [Guide + Examples]* https://blog.hubspot.com/marketing/brand-story

- *Social Media Marketing for Businesses* https://www.word-stream.com/social-media-marketing

- *13 Brilliant Customer Loyalty Program Examples* https://clever-tap.com/blog/customer-loyalty-program-examples/

- *7 Tips for Successful Small Business Content Marketing* https://neilpatel.com/blog/small-business-content-marketing/

- *10 Steps to Best-Practices Benchmarking - Quality Digest*https://www.qualitydigest.com/static/magazine/feb/bench.html

- *Principles of Total Quality Management in Small Business …* https://smallbusiness.chron.com/principles-total-quality-management-small-business-environment-4678.html

- *The Importance of Customer Feedback in Product …* https://medium.com/accredian/the-importance-of-customer-feed-back-in-product-development-44f674966884

- *Agile at Scale* https://hbr.org/2018/05/agile-at-scale

- *Why Core Values Matter (And How To Get Your Team …*https://www.forbes.com/sites/brentgleeson/2021/03/30/why-core-values-matter-and-how-to-get-your-team-excited-about-them/

- *4 case studies of companies with strong workplace cultures* https://testlify.com/studies-of-companies-with-good-workplace-cultures/#:~:text=The%20case%20studies%20of%20Google,cultures%20must%20evolve%20with%20it.

- *30 Employee Engagement Best Practices to Follow in 2023* https://www.lumapps.com/employee-engagement/employee-engagement-best-practices/

- *Does Your Company's Culture Reinforce Its Strategy and …* https://hbr.org/2022/06/does-your-companys-culture-reinforce-its-strategy-and-purpose

- *From Garage to Global: Inside the Explosive Growth of* … https://medium.com/@ibraheemjabbar/from-garage-to-global-inside-the-explosive-growth-of-tech-startups-160b190f51e9

- *How to Scale a Boutique Business Without Losing Its Charm* https://www.strategicadvisorboard.com/blog-posts/how-to-scale-a-boutique-business-without-losing-its-charm

- *101 Strategy & Transformation Case Studies of Consulting Firms* https://mark-bridges.medium.com/101-strategy-transformation-case-studies-of-consulting-firms-6857ffd6eb8f

- *Shopify vs. WooCommerce vs. Magento Comparison* https://amasty.com/blog/shopify-vs-woocommerce-vs-magento/

- *Business Exit Strategy: Definition, Examples, Best Types* https://www.investopedia.com/terms/b/business-exit-strategy.asp

- *How To Conduct a Small-Business Valuation* https://blog.hubspot.com/sales/small-business-valuation

- *Plan a Smooth Succession for Your Family Business* https://hbr.org/2022/09/plan-a-smooth-succession-for-your-family-business

- *How proactive CEOs build long-term sustainability strategies* https://www.coolset.com/academy/long-term-sustainability-strategies-ceo

· **Snapchat's Monetization Struggles:**

- How Snapchat's Business Model Struggles to Monetize https://www.investopedia.com/articles/investing/102216/snapchats-business-model-how-does-it-make-money.asp

- Why Snapchat's IPO Struggled to Monetize Its Users https://www.businessinsider.com/snapchat-ipo-how-its-struggling-to-monetize-2017-3

· **eBay's Global Expansion Missteps:**

- eBay's Expansion Failures in Japan: What Went Wrong? https://techcrunch.com/2017/08/23/ebays-expansion-failures-in-japan/

- How eBay Fumbled the International Market https://www.wsj.com/articles/how-ebay-fumbled-the-international-market-2019-05-21

· **Starbucks' Quality vs. Speed Dilemma:**

  - The Mistake Starbucks Made When It Grew Too Fast https://www.businessinsider.com/starbucks-mistake-rapid-growth-2019-1

  - How Starbucks Fixed Its Fast-Growth Strategy After Crisis https://hbr.org/2018/09/how-starbucks-fixed-its-fast-growth-strategy-after-crisis

· **Kodak's Failure to Embrace Digital Innovation:**

  - The Rise and Fall of Kodak: A Case Study in Innovation https://www.forbes.com/sites/forbestechcouncil/2014/06/09/the-rise-and-fall-of-kodak-a-case-study-in-innovation/

  - Kodak's Missed Opportunities and the Digital Photography Revolution https://www.businessinsider.com/kodaks-missed-opportunities-and-digital-photography-revolution-2012-4

· **Blockbuster's Missed Opportunity with Netflix:**

  - Blockbuster and Netflix: A Case Study in Missed Opportunities https://hbr.org/2019/02/blockbuster-and-netflix-a-case-study-in-missed-opportunities

  - The Fall of Blockbuster: How Netflix Beat the King of Video Rentals https://www.theverge.com/2019/4/15/18339751/blockbuster-netflix-history-competition-streaming

· **Airbnb's Initial Trust Issues:**

  - How Airbnb Built a $31 Billion Business by Tackling Trust Issues https://www.businessinsider.com/airbnb-built-31-billion-dollar-business-trust-issues-2018-2

- Airbnb's Growth Fueled by Focus on Trust and User Experience https://techcrunch.com/2015/01/23/airbnbs-focus-on-trust-and-user-experience/

· **WeWork's Reckless Expansion:**

- WeWork's Fall From Grace: A Cautionary Tale https://www.ft.com/content/74e2b9b0-e235-11e9-bfa4-b25f4c31f4f3

- How WeWork's IPO Failed to Live Up to the Hype https://www.nytimes.com/2019/09/16/technology/wework-ipo-failures.html

· **BlackBerry's Complacency in Innovation:**

- How BlackBerry Lost Its Mojo: Lessons From the Fall of an Icon https://www.theguardian.com/business/2016/feb/27/how-blackberry-lost-its-mojo-lessons-from-the-fall-of-an-icon

- BlackBerry's Decline and the End of a Mobile Revolution https://www.forbes.com/sites/forbestechcouncil/2017/01/31/blackberrys-decline-and-the-end-of-a-mobile-revolution/

- **Sara Blakely's Bootstrap Success:**

  o How Sara Blakely Built Spanx with Limited Capital https://www.forbes.com/sites/forbesbusiness-council/2021/04/06/how-sara-blakely-built-spanx-with-limited-capital/

  o From \$5,000 to a Billion-Dollar Business: The Story of Spanx https://www.businessinsider.com/sara-blakely-spanx-entrepreneur-journey-2021-4

- **Nick Woodman's GoPro Journey:**

  o GoPro's Beginnings: How Nick Woodman Turned an Idea into a Phenomenal Success https://www.businessinsider.com/how-nick-woodman-built-gopro-2014-6

- o The GoPro Origin Story: Nick Woodman's Journey from Vans to Cameras https://www.inc.com/magazine/201406/benjamin-c-winter/the-origin-of-gopro.html

- **Red Bull and GoPro Partnership:**

  - o The GoPro-Red Bull Partnership: Scaling through Collaboration https://www.forbes.com/sites/forbestechcouncil/2020/01/28/the-gopro-red-bull-partnership-scaling-through-collaboration/

  - o How GoPro and Red Bull's Partnership Changed the Game https://www.businessinsider.com/gopro-red-bull-partnership-2012-10

- **Google's Strategic Growth and Scalability:**

  - o Google's Growth Strategy: From Dorm Room to Global Empire https://hbr.org/2018/12/google-strategy-and-the-power-of-scale

  - o The Building Blocks of Google's Growth: PageRank and Scalability https://www.techradar.com/news/google-growth-strategy

- **Netflix's Technological Revolution:**

  - o How Netflix Used Technology to Disrupt the Entertainment Industry https://www.forbes.com/sites/forbestechcouncil/2021/04/15/how-netflix-used-technology-to-disrupt-the-entertainment-industry/

  - o The Rise of Netflix: Using Technology to Drive Entertainment Success https://www.businessinsider.com/how-netflix-used-technology-to-take-over-2018-1

- **Microsoft's Bill Gates and Team Strategy:**

  - o Bill Gates' Leadership Philosophy at Microsoft https://www.forbes.com/sites/forbestechcouncil/2019/11/05/bill-gates-leadership-philosophy-at-microsoft/

- o How Bill Gates Built the Microsoft Team That Changed the World https://www.inc.com/guides/2010/03/how-bill-gates-built-the-microsoft-team-that-changed-the-world.html

- **Google's Financial Management Strategy:**

  - o Google's Financial Strategy: Scaling through Strategic Reinvestment https://www.wsj.com/articles/googles-financial-strategy-scaling-through-strategic-reinvestment-2019-04-14

  - o How Google Managed Its Finances to Secure Long-Term Growth https://www.businessinsider.com/google-financial-strategy-2016-6

- **Coca-Cola's "Share a Coke" Campaign:**

  - o Coca-Cola's "Share a Coke" Campaign: Building Emotional Connections https://www.forbes.com/sites/forbesagencycouncil/2019/03/11/how-coca-colas-share-a-coke-campaign-built-emotional-connections/

  - o The Power of Personalization in Coca-Cola's Marketing Strategy https://www.businessinsider.com/how-coca-colas-share-a-coke-campaign-skyrocketed-sales-2014-7

- **LEGO's Reinvention and Community Focus:**

  - o How LEGO Reinvented Itself with Strong Storytelling and Fan Engagement https://www.forbes.com/sites/forbesbusinesscouncil/2020/07/30/how-lego-reinvented-itself-with-strong-storytelling-and-fan-engagement/

  - o The LEGO Brand Resurgence: How the Company Embraced Its Legacy to Achieve Success https://www.inc.com/guides/2014/12/how-lego-resurrected-its-brand-from-the-brink-of-bankruptcy.html

- **Zappos' Culture and Growth Strategy:**

- Zappos' Focus on Culture: How Tony Hsieh Built a Loyal Work-force https://www.inc.com/guides/2014/11/how-tony-hsieh-built-zappos-culture.html

- Zappos' Revolutionary Company Culture Strategy for Explosive Growth https://www.forbes.com/sites/forbeshumanre-sourcescouncil/2020/02/18/how-zappos-revolutionized-com-pany-culture-for-explosive-growth/